THE CHEF'S CANVAS

presented by

CUMMER MUSEUM OF ART & GARDENS

and **CARI SÁNCHEZ-POTTER**

foreword by

HOPE McMATH

photographs by

AGNES LOPEZ

CUMMER MUSEUM

ART | GARDENS | EDUCATION

First published in 2016 by the Cummer Museum of Art & Gardens
829 Riverside Avenue
Jacksonville, Florida 32204
cummermuseum.org

ISBN: 978-0-915135-17-2

Produced by the Cummer Museum of Art & Gardens
Concept by Hope McMath
Copy-edited and compiled by Cari Sánchez-Potter
Project managers Cari Sánchez-Potter and Emily Moody
Art copy written by Holly Keris
Artwork compiled by Kristen Zimmerman
Proof-read by Amber Sesnick, Kristen Zimmerman,
    Gabrielle Dean, and Dawn Zattau
Designed by Varick Rosete
Photography by Agnes Lopez
Styled by Emily Moody

Printed and bound in Jacksonville, Florida by The Hartley Press

Foreword

Hope McMath **THE ENGLISH GARDENS**

As Director of the Cummer Museum of Art & Gardens, one of my greatest thrills is to observe our visitors discovering the wonder, beauty, and history to be found in the works of art in our Collection and in the historic gardens that surround our campus. The objects and spaces that make up this Museum are at the heart of a mission to inspire and educate, but the most profound moments are when individuals find personal relevance in these experiences.

The Chef's Canvas was born from our commitment to find new ways for people to connect with works in the Collection. After many years of collaborating with contemporary artists, actors, musicians, dancers, historians, scientists, and others to reinterpret our Collection and Gardens through their eyes, hands, and hearts, we can now add chefs to that list. This publication shares the results of this latest exploration. The connections between the visual creations of painters, sculptors, printmakers, and landscape architects and the food creations of chefs, bartenders, and brewmasters are exciting to see...and taste. Whether the connections are aesthetic, cultural, or the result of a personal, often nostalgic connection, each pairing celebrates the beauty, interest, and abundance in the world around us.

This book is also a celebration of creativity across disciplines and the power of collaboration. I am profoundly grateful to those who stepped up to support this initiative. I am also thankful to the dozens of chefs, bartenders, and brewmasters in the North Florida region who shared their talent and time. There was something marvelous about watching culinary geniuses tour the Cummer Museum looking for the work of art that inspired them most deeply. The results of this process have inspired and surprised me.

It has been a thrill to collaborate with a remarkable group of creative professionals who each brought expertise, an incredible amount of time, and great sparkle to this project. I am especially appreciative for the work of Cari Sánchez-Potter, whose willingness to partner with the Museum on this project was immediate and enthusiastic. Thanks to Agnes Lopez for being more than a brilliant photographer, but someone who found beautiful connections between the Museum campus and the incredible dishes that were presented for to your lens. I am grateful to Varick Rosete for a design that elevates the art, the food, and the visual excellence that the Cummer Museum holds dear.

I am pleased to acknowledge the efforts of an extraordinary staff who have supported this project and the ongoing care, interpretation, and programmatic energy around the Cummer Museum's Collection day in and day out. I am especially grateful to Emily Moody, who expertly managed this project and brought the same passion and energy to *The Chef's Canvas* that she brings to our public programs throughout the year. For their willingness to find new ways of celebrating the history of art and always providing great content and quality, I thank Chief Curator Holly Keris and Registrar Kristen Zimmerman.

For the consistent support and enthusiasm of the Museum's Trustees, I extend special gratitude to Chair Ryan Schwartz and every member of our Board. Without the engagement and commitment to excellence of our Trustees, it would not be possible to create and sustain innovative and artful experiences like those exemplified by this publication and related programmatic initiatives.

I hope you will enjoy this feast for the senses and that this publication will inspire you to dine on the richness of the art of our collective history, experience the awe of the natural world around you, and explore the art of dining on great food in your own kitchen and at the table of others.

The Inspiration

Holly Keris **THE STEIN GALLERY**

New projects are always exciting, few more so than *The Chef's Canvas.* This is the first time since 2000 that the Cummer Museum of Art & Gardens is publishing a volume that encompasses the full scope of the Permanent Collection. Given the growth the Museum has experienced, thanks to many generous donors who have gifted works to the Collection and as a result of purchases made to commemorate the Museum's 50th anniversary, a new publication is a timely endeavor.

As opposed to a traditional museum guide, however, this book takes a different approach, and here's where the real excitement comes into play. Rather than providing only scholarly commentary, this publication seeks to uncover one of the Permanent Collection's most important functions— as a source of inspiration for our community. Even though we all have our personal favorites, looking at the Collection through someone else's eyes provides an opportunity to reconsider our assumptions and embrace new perspectives. Here, through the lens of some of Northeast Florida's most talented culinary creators, we can take a fresh look at some familiar favorites, not just considering facts and figures, but really thinking about how these works make us feel, how they connect with us in the present. I hope you will be inspired to revisit and reimagine the Cummer Museum, and bring some of this creative spirit into your kitchen.

The Memories

Emily Moody **THE JACOBSEN GALLERY**

As a Jacksonville native, the Cummer Museum of Art & Gardens held a special place in my heart long before I started working there. I have fond memories of attending events as a young girl with my grandmother, a former Museum volunteer. Now, many years later, I am the one planning the events and helping create memories for so many others.

Bringing *The Chef's Canvas* to life has been an exciting year-long adventure. Just as with anything at the Museum, whether it is an exhibition, educational tour, public program, or a book, it is important to keep each project "uniquely Cummer". This publication has accomplished that hands down! *The Chef's Canvas* highlights two very important elements that make up Jacksonville, the art and foodie cultures, and encompasses some of the finest works from the Museum's Permanent Collection while looking at them from a fresh perspective.

From the very first photoshoot with Tapa That to the last with Sweet Theory, the common goal among all the images was to ensure the true essence of the artwork was captured. Through carefully-selected serving vessels and thoughtfully-chosen backdrops, we celebrated the uniqueness of this project while ensuring the integrity of the artwork. We utilized many surfaces and textures of the Museum to tell a story where fine art meets fine food. Whether it was marble tiles and brick walkways or propping a plate above a reflecting pool in the Italian Garden or on a boxwood in the English Garden, it was a special experience to highlight spaces where the Museum's founder, Ninah Cummer, spent so much time.

As you are reading through *The Chef's Canvas*, I invite you to look deeper at the images (although some correlations are much more literal than others) with the idea that you will spot the unique, thoughtful details and special connections between fine art and each culinary counterpart in this innovative publication. I truly hope this book will stir up old memories and help you make new ones, whether it's in your kitchen or at the Cummer Museum.

The Journey

Cari Sánchez-Potter **THE LANE GALLERY**

The journey of producing *The Chef's Canvas* began when Hope McMath and Holly Keris reached out to me with the revolutionary idea of pairing art works from the Museum's Collection with prominent members of our local culinary scene. I could not contain my enthusiasm for the concept, and the project has proven to be unique and groundbreaking in every respect.

Our local chefs, food truck owners, bartenders, and brewers all shared my enthusiasm for the cookbook from the very beginning. We invited them to the Museum to choose an artwork that personally inspired them, and the choices they made comprise the soul of the book. For some, certain pieces reminded them of a favorite childhood dish or a transformative travel experience. Others took on the challenge of a literal interpretation and recreated a painting in food form. Some responded to colors, shapes, or a general feeling evoked by the art they chose.

Once each participant was paired with an artwork, they went to work crafting dishes that are a culinary expression of that art. Each then wrote a statement that speaks to the connection between their recipe and their chosen painting, print, garden, or sculpture. Many of these statements are surprisingly heartfelt. They interpret art using food as a lens and show us there are endless ways we can experience and appreciate the Museum's wonderful Collection.

The recipes range from a colorful salsa that requires no cooking and just fifteen minutes of prep time to an elaborate carpaccio consisting of seven individually concocted elements of immense refinement. This diversity represents all that is best in both art and food. In culinary art and in fine art, sometimes simplicity strikes the biggest cord by evoking a feeling of comfort, satisfaction, or familiarity. In other instances, showing off impeccable technique accumulated over years of study, practice, and implementation is the best way to convey meaning and excite the senses.

This incredibly collaborative project mirrors the unique cooperative spirit found in Northeast Florida's cultural community. We are enriched by the ability of our region's creative talent to set their egos aside in order to help each other achieve goals that benefit our cultural scene as a whole. Without this community-minded approach and the visionary leadership of the Cummer Museum, *The Chef's Canvas* could not have come to fruition. The cookbook was a revolutionary idea when brought to me by the Museum. Now, after going through the process of bringing this project to life, it feels like a natural progression for our City. We are on our way to being recognized as a culinary and cultural force across the Southeast, and *The Chef's Canvas* provides a mouthwatering snapshot of our journey.

The Passion

Jamey Evoniuk **THE CAFÉ PATIO**

Great art is fueled by passion. It has the ability to unify people by connecting them to different times, cultures, and places. It tells a story, nourishes a community, and feeds the creative spirit.

Likewise, great food is also the product of passion. Food has the power to unify people and connect us to different times, introduce us to new cultures, and take us to different places—figuratively, only if you've never experienced a meal that is out of this world. When we take the time to come around the table to share a meal, we tell stories, nourish our bodies, and feed our collective, creative spirit.

Great food, like art, is the result of artistic skill and an example of imagination made tangible. It can be as stunning in its ingenuity as it is in its form and flavor. That's why we call it Culinary Art. *The Chef's Canvas* is a testament to the Cummer Museum of Art & Gardens' ability to see beyond its own walls and understand that an artist's canvas exists in countless forms. The world's most beloved cities are culturally rich—not only in art institutions and resources, but with vibrant and diverse culinary scenes. The chefs who came together to create this book add to the fabric of our community, and are pivotal in changing the perception of Jacksonville as a city that can be great, to a city that is already great. I am thankful to be part of a community that not only has the talent to create this collection of art, but which will embrace this project with ravenous enthusiasm.

The Concert (A Musical Party)

BOUILLABAISSE: MIDDLE NECK CLAMS, DIVER SCALLOPS, ROCK SHRIMP, LOBSTER, HEIRLOOM CHERRY TOMATOES, BLACK GARLIC-SAFFRON BROTH, GRILLED BAGUETTE

Jamey Evoniuk **CANDY APPLE CAFÉ**

Serves 4

Pinch saffron
4 cups sauvignon blanc
2 – 12 ounce lobster tails, raw
8 – U/10 scallops
12 middle neck clams
½ pound rock shrimp
24 mussels
1 pint heirloom cherry tomatoes
½ pound butter
1 tablespoon chives, snipped
1 tablespoon parsley, lightly chopped
1 tablespoon chiffonade basil
1 French baguette
Fried leeks
3 cloves black garlic, thinly sliced
Salt and pepper

In a medium saucepot, steep the saffron in the white wine on low heat for 15 minutes.

Meanwhile, with kitchen shears, carefully split the top shell of the lobsters and remove meat. Split the tails in half so you have four pieces.

Season the scallops and lobster with salt and pepper. Heat a large braising pan over medium-high heat and sear the seafood, starting with the scallops and lobster then adding clams, rock shrimp, mussels, and cherry tomatoes. Add the saffron-infused wine, cover, and cook for one minute. Add the butter and herbs and cook until emulsified. Discard any unopened mussels and clams, then taste broth and adjust seasoning if needed.

Remove the seafood and place in a large serving bowl. Boil broth for no longer than one minute to slightly reduce, then pour over seafood.

Slice baguette on the bias and brush with butter. Lightly grill both sides. Garnish soup with fried leeks, black garlic, and grilled baguette.

Scenes of music parties, like this one by Theodoor Rombouts, were common among Flemish artists of the 17th century. Here, Rombouts used dramatic lighting to highlight various features of the musicians, who gather around a central table. These features – ear, nose, hand, and eye – correspond to four of the five senses. Rombouts studied the work of Italian artist Caravaggio (1571 – 1610) when he lived in Rome. Rombouts' use of bright light and deep shadows recalls Caravaggio's similar dramatic lighting effects.

❝

This painting portrays a music party, celebrating the five senses and there is no better dish than a bouillabaisse to equal this. To fully enjoy bouillabaisse, a diner must use all her senses: taking in the beauty of its presentation, the feel of breaking the clam shells and dipping the baguette into the broth, the smell of the seafood steeped in the aromatic broth, and the taste of all ingredients as they come together. Much like a concert, each ingredient has a singular and harmonic beauty that, while delicious on its own, is taken to an even greater level when enjoyed in harmony with the others. I intentionally selected a dish with a heavy seafood focus because I believe that music, the ocean, and food have a supernatural ability to take people to a different place.

—Jamey Evoniuk
The Concert (A Musical Party)

Pieter Aertsen
Netherlandish, 1507/08 – 1575
The Parable of the Marriage Feast
1550 – 1554
Oil on panel
Purchased with funds from the Cummer Council
AP.1965.12.1

*Pieter Aertsen, born and trained in Amsterdam, spent much
of his career working in Antwerp. Many of his large-scale
religious scenes were destroyed during the Beeldenstorm of
1566, a period of political and religious upheaval throughout
Belgium, the Netherlands, and Luxembourg. The Parable of the
Marriage Feast, a rare surviving work, depicts the entire parable
as outlined in Matthew (22:1-14). A king invited his subjects to
celebrate the wedding of his son. When none arrived, the king
commanded his servants to collect "both bad and good" so the
celebration could commence. However, the king noticed one
among the crowd not dressed for the occasion and had him
banished. The parable ends with the words, "many are called,
but few are chosen."*

The Parable of the Marriage Feast

ROSEMARY LEMON LEG OF LAMB WITH JERUSALEM ARTICHOKES AND
RAINBOW CARROTS SERVED WITH SAUCE BORDELAISE

Celestia Mobley **POTTER'S HOUSE SOUL FOOD BISTRO**

Serves 6 – 8

ROSEMARY LEMON LEG OF LAMB

3 lemons, zested and juiced
3 sprigs rosemary, leaves removed
3 sprigs thyme, leaves removed
6 cloves garlic, chopped
2 tablespoons salt
1 tablespoon Spanish paprika
½ teaspoon freshly ground pepper
1 cup extra virgin olive oil
1 leg of lamb

Place the lemon zest, lemon juice, rosemary, thyme, garlic, salt, paprika, pepper, and olive oil in a food processor. Finely process all ingredients together. Massage the mixture into the leg of lamb and marinate overnight, turning occasionally.

Preheat oven to 300 degrees.

Place lamb in a large roasting pan. Add 2 cups of water to the pan and cover tightly with aluminum foil. Bake for five hours, until lamb is pull-apart tender. Allow the meat to rest for 30 minutes.

Lamb will be extremely tender so transfer carefully to a platter. Reserve pan juices.

Serve lamb with Bordelaise Sauce, Jerusalem Artichokes, and Rainbow Carrots.

BORDELAISE SAUCE

1 cup dry red wine
2 teaspoons cracked black pepper
1 sprig fresh thyme
1 cup pan juices
2 tablespoons butter
Salt to taste

Combine wine, pepper, thyme, and pan juices in a medium saucepan. Cook over medium-high heat until slightly reduced. Strain sauce through a fine mesh strainer and add it back to the pan. Stir in butter and season to taste with salt.

JERUSALEM ARTICHOKES AND RAINBOW CARROTS

1 pound rainbow carrots
½ pound Jerusalem artichokes
3 tablespoons olive oil
1 teaspoon kosher salt
½ teaspoon black pepper

Preheat oven to 350 degrees.

Toss all ingredients together and place in a baking pan. Roast for 20 minutes.

The Parable of the Marriage Feast *is Pieter Aertsen's depiction of the story Jesus told about the King who invited people to his son's wedding. I chose to depict the story using a leg of lamb because Jesus was known as the Lamb of God. I also chose Jerusalem Artichokes because the feast of the Passover took place in Jerusalem yearly. Lastly I chose a red wine sauce because Jesus' first miracle was turning water into wine.*

—*Celestia Mobley*
The Parable of the Marriage Fest

Light Squares I

LOBSTER JAXRIBBEAN: MACADAMIA CRUSTED LOBSTER TAIL WITH GASTRIQUE

Chris Dickerson **CORNER TACO**

Serves 2

MACADAMIA CRUSTED LOBSTER TAIL

½ *cup* roasted, salted macadamia nuts, chopped
¼ *cup* panko breadcrumbs
Pinch ground datil pepper (or cayenne)
1 *tablespoon* unsalted butter, melted
2 - 8 *ounce* lobster tails
¼ *cup* Wondra, rice flour, or all-purpose flour
Salt, to taste

Pulse macadamias in a food processor until they are the size of peas. Do not over-pulse or you'll have macadamia nut butter.

Combine nuts, panko, ground datil, and butter in a bowl. Chill for at least 1 hour to set. Crust can be made several days in advance.

Preheat oven to 425 degrees.

Remove lobster meat from the shell by making an incision along the length and several horizontal cuts in order to free meat from shell.

Place a wooden skewer through the tail so the meat won't curl. Snip one end of the skewer so the tail will fit in a pan. Season lobster lightly with salt and dust lightly with Wondra, rice flour, or all-purpose flour. Heat a heavy-bottomed pan over medium-high heat and sear lobster on both sides until a caramel color appears.

Place about ¼ of the macadamia crust on top of each tail and bake until golden, about 8 minutes.

GASTRIQUE

2 *cups* of your favorite citrus juice
Approximately 1 teaspoon white distilled vinegar
1 *teaspoon* (or more) unbleached cane sugar

Add all ingredients to a saucepan and reduce until "nape" consistency, or a consistency that would cling to the back of a wooden spoon without clumping.

Citrus juice works really well for this gastrique. Try blending lemon with some orange, grapefruit, and pineapple. I like pre-made juice blends such as "Morning Blend" with papaya, pear, and pineapple.

Essentially a gastrique is a refined sweet and sour sauce. Keep the sweet/sour dynamic in mind when adding the vinegar and sugar. You will need more vinegar for sweeter juices like orange, less for more tart juices like lemon. Same goes for the sugar: You won't need much, if any, for sweeter juices like orange, but you'll need more for tarter juices like lemon.

To serve:

Spoon gastrique onto a plate and gently place lobster tail on top.

"

This painting is all about light. Gastriques are a beautiful way to celebrate light and undertone. Light Squares *made me think of the Florida Keys and the food movement there known as "Floribbean." This recipe is an homage to that.*

—Chris Dickerson
Light Squares I

Trevor Bell
British, b. 1930
Light Squares I
1985
Acrylic on canvas
Gift of the Regency Group
AG.1991.2.1

A recipient of international awards including the 1959 Paris Biennale International Painting Prize and a Gregory Fellowship at Leeds University, Trevor Bell received additional recognition after a large traveling retrospective of his work in Scotland, Ireland, and England in 1970 and a solo exhibition at Washington, D.C.'s Corcoran Gallery in 1974. He became a professor of graduate-level painting at Florida State University in Tallahassee in 1976 and remained in this country for 20 years before returning to England, where he continues to exhibit widely. Bell's works are in the permanent collections of the Tate Gallery, the British Museum, and the Victoria and Albert Museum. His works illuminate the dichotomy and harmony between vibrating color and perceived immediacy of expression, within the parameters of a more formal structure.

© Trevor Bell

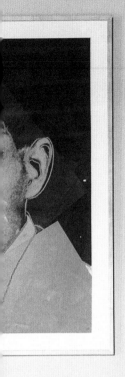
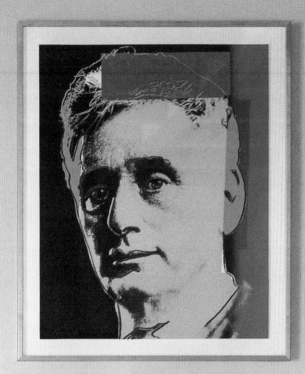

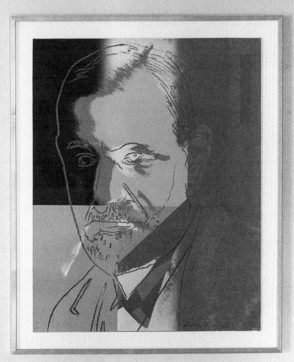

Andy Warhol
American, 1928 – 1987
Ten Portraits of Jews of the Twentieth Century
1980
Silkscreen on paper
Gift of Mr. and Mrs. Daniel M. Edelman
AG.2012.4.1 – 10

Andy Warhol was an instrumental figure in the development of American Pop Art, which used images from mass media and materials from commercial production as inspiration for a new style of art. However, Warhol turned away from contemporary culture in the series Ten Portraits of Jews of the Twentieth Century. The series highlights Jewish leaders in the areas of literature, film, philosophy, music, medicine, law, and science, including French actress Sarah Bernhardt (1844 – 1923), the first Jewish justice of the United States Supreme Court Louis Brandeis (1856 – 1941), physicist Albert Einstein (1897 – 1955), psychoanalyst Sigmund Freud (1856 – 1939), and comedians, the Marx Brothers.

66

People often ask me what my favorite dish is, or what is my specialty.

My answer? I don't have any. The food I choose to cook is generally humble

and comforting without too much manipulation of perfect ingredients.

Color, smell, taste, and feel stimulate all the senses and inspiration comes

from deeply felt experiences, sometimes based on current situations or

memories engraved in our souls.

My cooking is a reflection of a lifetime of experiences, seasons,

environments, and temporary states of mind. Though I take my inspiration

from fresh ingredients at their peak, cross-cultural influences play a big

part in my creations. They are connections to my heritage and past

working experiences.

—Eddy Escriba
Ten Portraits of Jews of
the Twentieth Century

———

Ten Portraits of Jews of the Twentieth Century

MATZO BALL CHICKEN CONSOMMÉ

Eddy Escriba **UPTOWN KITCHEN + BAR**

Serves 8 – 10

CONSOMMÉ

1 small chicken (2 ½ – 3 lbs), cut in half
2 quarts homemade chicken broth, or low
   sodium store-bought
2 quarts water
5 black peppercorns
2 bay leaves
1 yellow onion
2 celery stalks
2 medium carrots
2 cloves garlic
3 sprigs fresh thyme
3 sprigs parsley
Kosher salt, to taste

Place chicken halves in a large stock pot along with chicken broth, water, peppercorns, and bay leaves. Heat over medium heat until the broth starts to simmer. Reduce heat to low and maintain a low simmer for 1 ½ hours, occasionally skimming any foam that rises to the top. Be careful to not "boil" the broth, as it will emulsify and become cloudy.

Using tongs, remove chicken from the stock. Remove breast meat from the ribs and reserve.

Add the onion, celery stalks, and carrots to stock and continue to simmer for another hour, skimming occasionally.

Add the garlic, thyme, and parsley and let the herbs steep in the stock for 30 minutes. Strain the broth through a fine mesh sieve and discard all solids.

Cool the broth in an ice bath or in the refrigerator until the chicken fat solidifies on top. Skim the schmaltz (chicken fat) from the top of the broth and reserve for matzo balls.

MATZO BALLS

1 cup matzo meal
4 large eggs
6 ounces of schmaltz (reserved chicken fat
   from consommé)
¼ teaspoon kosher salt
¼ teaspoon black pepper
1 tablespoon baking powder

Mix all ingredients thoroughly in a large bowl. Cover and refrigerate for two hours. The mixture will expand.

Form the matzo mixture into golf ball-sized balls. Moisten the palms of your hands with water so the matzo balls are smooth on the outside with no cracks.

To finish and serve:

8 cups chicken consommé
1 celery stalk, cut into small batons
1 carrot, cut into small batons
1 zucchini and/or summer squash, cut into
   small batons
1 cup snow peas, julienned, for garnish
Fresh dill, for garnish

Cook matzo balls in low simmering broth for 20 minutes. During the last few minutes of cooking, add celery, carrot, and zucchini. Add reserved chicken breast meat to soup, if desired. Garnish soup with snow peas and a sprig of fresh dill.

Abstraction

CRISPY MERENGUE, MACARONS, MANGO GEL, RASPBERRY GELEE,
STRAWBERRY YOGURT MOUSSE, WHITE CHOCOLATE LIME MOUSSE

Sheldon Millett **SALT RESTAURANT**

CRISPY MERINGUE

50 *milliliters* egg whites
50 *grams* sugar
50 *grams* powdered sugar, sifted

Preheat oven to 200 degrees.

Whip egg whites and sugar to stiff peaks. Fold in powdered sugar. Pipe to desired shape on a silpat and bake meringues, checking at 15 minutes and removing when meringues easily release from the silpat.

MACARONS

100 *grams* egg whites
100 *grams* sugar
100 *grams* almond flour
150 *grams* powdered sugar

Whisk egg whites and sugar together until soft medium peaks form. Add food coloring.

In a separate bowl, sift almond flour and powdered sugar together and fold into egg whites.

Pipe onto a silpat with #804 tip and let rest around 30 minutes.

While resting, preheat oven to 275 degrees. Bake macarons for 14 minutes, rotating sheet halfway through.

MANGO GEL

500 *grams* mango puree
75 *grams* sugar
5 *grams* agar agar powder

Boil all ingredients together in a small pot. Remove from heat and cool completely. Refrigerate for at least 4 hours. Using a hand blender, blend mixture together.

RASPBERRY GELEE

500 *grams* raspberry puree
10 gelatin sheets

In a small saucepan, bring raspberry puree to a simmer. Bloom gelatin and add to puree. Whisk until gelatin is dissolved.

Pour raspberry mixture onto a ½ sheet pan lined with acetate and refrigerate until set.

STRAWBERRY YOGURT MOUSSE

110 *grams* sugar
300 *grams* strawberry marmalade
5 egg yolks
500 *grams* yogurt
18 gelatin sheets
590 *grams* strawberry puree
930 *grams* heavy cream

Whisk sugar and strawberry marmalade together, then whisk in egg yolks followed by yogurt.

Bloom gelatin and add to strawberry puree. Keep warm on bain marie.

Whisk cream until soft peaks form.

With mixer on low speed, add warm gelatin mixture to strawberry yogurt mixture. Fold cream into strawberry mixture to form a batter.

Divide batter onto two flat sheet pans lined with silpats.

WHITE CHOCOLATE LIME MOUSSE

7 egg yolks
85 *grams* sugar
7 *sheets* gelatin
125 *grams* heavy cream
312 *grams* white chocolate
½ *teaspoon* lime oil
1 *piece* lime zest
750 *grams* heavy cream
100 *grams* lime juice

(CONTINUED)

In a mixer fitted with whisk attachment, whip yolks and sugar to ribbon stage.

Bloom the sheet gelatin in ice water.

Bring 125 grams heavy cream to a boil, then pour over the white chocolate. Add the lime oil and lime zest and mix until chocolate is melted.

Drain the bloomed gelatin of all water and add to the white chocolate mixture.

Whip remaining 750 grams cream in mixer to soft peak.

Add the white chocolate mixture to the whipped yolks mixture until incorporated. Fold yolks into the soft whip cream and add lime juice. Pour mousse into sheet pan and freeze until set. Cut to desired shape.

Rolph Scarlett
American, born in Canada, 1889 – 1984
Abstraction
c. 1934
Oil on canvas
Purchased with funds from the Morton R. Hirschberg Bequest and gifts from Diane DeMell Jacobsen, Ph.D. in loving memory of her husband Thomas H. Jacobsen and James and Diane Burke in memory of Thomas H. Jacobsen
AP.2005.1.1

Rolph Scarlett had a varied career in the arts, working as a theatrical designer and jeweler. He experimented with several artistic styles before committing to abstraction. Scarlett's work appealed to Hilla Rebay and Solomon Guggenheim, who were forming the collection of the Museum of Non-Objective Painting (now the Solomon R. Guggenheim Museum). Not only did they purchase more than 60 of Scarlett's paintings for the new museum, they also hired Scarlett as chief lecturer.

"

Abstraction was created by a Canadian artist from Guelf, Ontario, which is very close to my home town. I loved the painting and, when I read he was from Canada, I had to make a dessert.

I had fun creating an abstract dessert to go along with Abstraction. *Our idea was to feature Florida flavors of citrus, strawberries, and tropical fruits. As a Canadian, these are the fruits we go for first when we come to Florida, so I thought it was fitting to use them. When we put the plate together, I think the painting and the picture complement each other.*

Abstraction means reducing something down to its essential ingredients, taking a fresh look, and reordering the structure. It's really a powerful way of looking at your life and an inspiring way to create beautiful things.

—Sheldon Millett
Abstraction

The Portrait of Princess Pauline Borghèse and the Baroness de Mathisse *is an exquisite painting by René-Théodore Berthon. It depicts the leisurely life of a wealthy woman in the early 18th century. My family is of French heritage and I have been trained in a Classic French kitchen. It seemed fitting that I would gravitate to all things French. Breads, cakes, and pastries are in my blood. This portrait makes me dream of making eclairs and Parisian macarons for the artist and his subjects.*

—*Mallorie Finnell*
Portrait of Princess Pauline Borghèse
and the Baroness de Mathisse

René-Théodore Berthon
French, 1776 – 1859
**Portrait of Princess Pauline Borghèse and
the Baroness de Mathisse**
c. 1810
Oil on canvas
Purchased with funds from the Cummer Council
AP.2002.2.1

Much like today's celebrities, Princess Pauline Borghèse and her friend, the Baroness de Mathisse, model the latest fashions in René-Théodore Berthon's large painting. The youngest sister of Napoleon Bonaparte, Pauline was recognized as a fashion trendsetter and legendary beauty, while also gaining a reputation as one of Europe's most scandalous women. Here, she and her friend pose with their shawls, the true markers of high end fashion. Shawls and other mid- and near-East woven goods were brought to France by Napoleon's officers, and they quickly became fashionably exotic accessories. Their bright colors and decorative patterning brought lightness and visual interest to the subdued styling of Empire gowns.

Portrait of Princess Pauline Borghèse and the Baroness de Mathisse

RED VELVET CHEESECAKE

Mallorie Finnell **B THE BAKERY FOR BB'S AND BISCOTTI'S**

Serves 10

RED VELVET CAKE

1 cup vegetable shortening
2 eggs
1 ½ cups sugar
1 teaspoon cocoa powder
2 ounces red food coloring
2 ½ cups cake flour
1 teaspoon salt
1 cup buttermilk
1 teaspoon vanilla extract
1 teaspoon baking soda
1 teaspoon vinegar

Preheat oven to 350 degrees.

In the bowl of a mixer, cream together the shortening, eggs, and sugar. In a separate small bowl, mix together the cocoa and food coloring. Add this paste to the shortening mixture.

Sift the flour and salt together. Add to the batter alternately with the buttermilk in 3 additions. Add the vanilla extract. Fold in the baking soda and vinegar.

Pour the batter into 2 greased 10-inch cake pans. Bake for 30 minutes, or until an inserted cake tester comes out clean. Cool completely.

WHITE CHOCOLATE CHEESECAKE

1 ¼ pounds cream cheese, divided
4 ounces granulated sugar
2 whole eggs
1 teaspoon lemon zest
1 teaspoon lemon juice
⅛ tablespoon vanilla extract
1 ounce unsalted butter
⅓ cup sour cream
¼ pound Hershey's white chocolate chips

Preheat oven to 200 degrees. Spray 10-inch spring form cake pan with cooking spray.

Place half of cream cheese in a mixer and beat on low speed for 3 to 5 minutes. Add sugar and continue to mix on low speed. Scrape. Continue to mix on low speed for a minute. Increase mixer to speed two and beat for 2 minutes. On low speed, gradually add the eggs, lemon zest, juice, and vanilla extract. Continue to mix until mostly combined. Scrape again. Mix on low speed for approximately 2 minutes.

Combine the remaining cream cheese, butter, sour cream, and white chocolate in a large container and melt in microwave until smooth and creamy.

(CONTINUED)

Add the chocolate mixture to batter in two or three batches, and mix just until combined. Scrape and mix on low speed until combined. Pour into prepared cake pan. Bake for 1 hour 15 minutes, or until set firm. Cool completely.

WHITE CHOCOLATE GANACHE

1 ¼ cups heavy cream
⅓ pound Hershey's white chocolate chips
⅓ pound cocoa barry blanc satin pistols
½ pound butter, softened

Heat cream to the scalding point. Remove from heat and add the chocolate. Whisk together until smooth and all chocolate is melted. Add butter to mixture and continue to whisk until blended. Cool, cover, and refrigerate.

WHITE CHOCOLATE GANACHE FROSTING

2 ½ cups heavy cream
3 cups white chocolate ganache (from above recipe)
½ cup powdered sugar

In a small mixer, whip together all ingredients. Whip to moderately stiff peaks. Use immediately. *Do not over whip.*

To assemble, place cheese cake layer on the base of your cake plate. Layer with white chocolate ganache frosting then add a layer of red velvet cake. Repeat with another layer of white chocolate ganache frosting and red velvet cake. Cover the sides and top of cake with remaining white chocolate ganache frosting. Garnish with white chocolate shavings.

Severin Roesen
American, born in Germany,
c. 1815 – 1872
Still Life with Flowers, Fruit and Bird's Nest
c. 1865
Oil on canvas
Gift of Diane DeMell Jacobsen, Ph.D. in loving memory of her husband Thomas H. Jacobsen
AG.2003.2.1

Highly regarded for his sumptuous still lifes, German-born Severin Roesen transformed the genre in this country when he emigrated in 1848. His lavish compositions juxtaposed with more austere works common in the early 19th century. Inspired by 17th- and 18th-century Dutch compositions, Roesen's bountiful combinations of fruits, flowers, and other objects like the glass bowl and bird's nest seen here also speak to the perceived abundance of America's natural resources and the prevailing idea that this country's success was preordained by God. Although little definitive is known about his early life, it is likely that Roesen trained as a porcelain painter in Germany, as evidenced by his incredible attention to detail.

Still Life with Flowers, Fruit and Bird's Nest

JUNE BUG

Casey Shelton
DOS GATOS

1 ounce fresh lemon juice
Freshly muddled mango and cucumber
Sugar, to balance
1 ½ ounces gin
½ ounce June liqueur or St. Germaine
Cucumber strap, to garnish
Cayenne pepper, to garnish

Shake and strain over rocks. Garnish with a cucumber and a dusting
of cayenne pepper.

*The piece contains beautiful bright colors in the
foreground with subtle undertones of earthiness in the
background. I wanted the cocktail to mimic this balance,
so I started with vibrant flavors found in lemon and
mango, then used the cucumber to provide an earthy
contrast to those bold flavors. I then took a very floral gin
and a sweeter botanical liqueur to offset the spice from
the cayenne pepper, and the result is this deliciously
sweet and spicy cocktail.*

MOTHER LADY BOPPARD

Marlon Hall
CANDY APPLE CAFE

2 ounces Nolets gin
½ ounce Lairds applejack
½ ounce lemon juice
½ ounce simple syrup
½ ounce grenadine
1 egg white
Edible flowers, to garnish

Combine all ingredients and vigorously dry shake for 45 seconds
(shake without ice to emulsify egg white). Add large ice cubes. Shake for
another 10 seconds to chill drink without over-diluting. Strain into a
coupe glass and garnish with edible flowers.

*As a bartender, it is easy to draw inspiration from
the changing seasons, bold new flavors and textures,
and other culinary stimuli. After viewing this still life
painting, I could immediately imagine the wonderfully
fragrant bouquet. I could imagine spring in full bloom,
light airy temperatures, and the sounds of nature;
Mother Nature at her most fertile. I also found I wanted
to incorporate the fact that it is an oil painting and
wanted to mimic its smooth texture. My cocktail had to
be light in body and texture, floral, and with a balanced
savory taste. Gin!*

ROESEN COLLINS

Zach Lynch
THE ICE PLANT

1 ½ ounces St. Augustine gin
¾ ounce lemon juice
½ ounce creme de peche
½ ounce strawberry syrup
1 egg white
4 dashes orange flower water
Peychauds, to top
2 ounces champagne, to top
Edible herb flowers, to garnish

Place all the ingredients in a shaker. Shake with one ice cube to break the proteins of the egg white. Then shake with ice and strain into Collins glass. Top with Peychauds bitters, champagne, and edible flowers.

The inspiration for the Roesen Collins came quite literally from the items depicted in the painting. The bird's nest with egg inspired the use of an egg white, the floral arrangement translated into the use of a botanical gin with fragrant orange flower water, and the strawberries led to the use of strawberry syrup which contributes color to the cocktail. I can almost taste the flavors of this cocktail whenever I look at the painting.

THE HUMMINGBIRD ROYALE

Blair Redington
THE PARLOUR AT GRAPE AND GRAIN EXCHANGE

2 ounces Nolets Gin
¾ ounce Elderflower Liqueur
¾ ounce lime
¼ ounce Stregga
2 strawberries
Handful of raspberries
Ginger Beer, to top off
Lavender Bitters, to top off

Shake all ingredients and strain over ice. Top off with Ginger Beer and Lavender Bitters.

The painting is fresh and floral. The bright red colors made me want to stick to red fruits like strawberries and raspberries. I chose a floral gin in Nolets and also used Elderflower liquor and topped it with lavender bitters to add the extra sense as you go into your first sip.

VIOLET'S GAZE

Kurt Rogers
SIDECAR

1 ¼ ounces Kappa Pisco
½ ounce Giffards creme de violet
½ ounce fresh lime juice
½ ounce fresh grapefruit juice
½ ounce simple syrup
1 dash of Abbotts bitters
1 egg white
Angostura bitters, to garnish
Chili powder, to garnish

Combine all ingredients in a cocktail shaker and dry shake for 10 seconds. Add ice and cold shake for another 10 seconds. Double strain into a chilled glass. Garnish with Angostora bitters and chili powder.

I'm not going to lie; at first I was having a hard time finding inspiration from this painting. I tried looking up the artist and maybe trying to find some inspiration from his life. Nothing. It wasn't until I went to the Museum and saw it in person that it hit me like a ton of bricks. The little nest of eggs was calling to me; I'm a sucker for an egg drink. But, what was really getting me was the color violet in the corner, all by itself, and making a strong statement. My great-grandmother's name was Violet, and she had to be one of the strongest people I have ever met. I miss her greatly, and I wanted to dedicate this to her memory. Thank you for all the life lessons, and you were right, hard work does pay off.

Kitchen at Mount Vernon

PEACH AND CORNMEAL TARTE TATIN

Meredith Corey-Disch and Sarah Bogdanovitch **COMMUNITY LOAVES**

Serves 8

THE PASTRY

1 cup all-purpose flour
1 cup stone ground cornmeal
1 teaspoon salt
1 cup cold unsalted butter, diced
⅓ cup cold water

Combine flour, cornmeal, and salt in bowl. Add butter and mix so that butter is coated with flour. Pour out onto a work surface and roll out with a rolling pin. Once all butter is flattened use a dough knife to bring your ingredients back to the center and roll them out again. Repeat this one more time, and then bring ingredients back to the center and make a well. Add cold water and use a dough knife to cut it into the butter/flour mixture. The amount of water you need will depend upon your flour and cornmeal, so make sure you only add enough water so that everything sticks together without getting so sticky it will stick to your rolling pin. Roll out one last time.

Place your dough in a bowl in the refrigerator. Allow to rest for one hour. If you are working in a hot kitchen and your butter is melting, be sure to stop what you are doing during any of these steps and give the dough some time in the fridge to harden.

Bring dough back onto the work surface and roll out into a rectangle. Fold it in on itself in thirds, like a letter, and turn it 90 degrees. Repeat and then roll it into the size of a 9-inch round cast iron pot. Place dough on a plate or baking sheet and place in refrigerator.

THE FILLING

½ cup sugar (I use evaporated cane juice, a little darker than regular granulated sugar)
¼ cup butter
6 peaches, firm, cut into quarters and stones removed

Preheat oven to 350 degrees.

Place sugar and butter in a cast iron pot over medium heat. Heat, stirring only once or twice, until sugar has dissolved and the mixture has started to brown slightly. Once it has begun to brown, place peach sections in the caramelizing sugar and butter, skin side down, side by side. You should have enough peaches to tightly fill the pan. Cook for another five minutes. Place rolled out pastry over the peaches, tucking it in between the peaches and the pan.

Place in hot oven and bake for 30 minutes to an hour, depending on your oven. Tarte will be done when the liquid is bubbling up around the edges, the crust has darkened, and all the layers of pastry are separated when cut into.

Allow to cool in the pan for about five minutes, then use a knife to loosen the edges of the crust and flip it out onto a serving dish.

Enjoy warm, served with fresh whipped cream or vanilla ice cream.

"

I love food histories and farming traditions. On George Washington's plantation, Mt. Vernon, wheat was grown for overseas markets and corn was ground into meal for consumption on the plantation.

This painting depicts a slave sitting in front of the main hearth, where a dish such as this would first be caramelized over an open fire, then baked in a dutch oven with coals. I am using butter, stone fruits, sugar, and white flour; ingredients that likely would not have been available to the slaves of any Southern plantation. I also use a large amount of cornmeal, almost half the dry weight of the puff pastry. It brings flavor, texture, and color, but also, pays homage to the slaves who would have been given cornmeal as one of the staples of their diets.

This is a simple dish, but by using stone ground cornmeal and fresh, seasonal fruit it is able to convey some of the main themes of Mt. Vernon's food history.

—*Meredith Corey-Disch and Sarah Bogdanovitch*
Kitchen at Mount Vernon

Eastman Johnson
American, 1824 – 1906
Kitchen at Mount Vernon
c. 1857
Oil on panel
Bequest of Ninah M. H. Cummer
C.0.117.1

In 1857, on the eve of the American Civil War, painter Eastman Johnson visited Mount Vernon, the Virginia home of George Washington (1732 – 1799). Johnson painted at least six iterations of the estate's kitchen before 1865, each showing an enslaved African American woman and small children. Twenty-six slaves remained on the plantation at the time of Johnson's visit, and his works reflect the degree to which the once-great estate had declined since the president's death. The year after Johnson's visit, a group of women organized the Mount Vernon Ladies' Association, which purchased and restored the property. The plantation remains under their care today.

Edgar Degas
French, 1834 – 1917
Scene with Ballerinas
c. 1890
Charcoal and pastel on paper
Bequest of Ruth P. Phillips
AG.2005.5.1

Although associated today with the Impressionists, French artist Edgar Degas considered himself a Realist, part of a movement ushered in following the Revolution of 1848 that sought to capture truthful representations of contemporary life. Degas focused his efforts on leisure activities, such as horse races, concerts, urban cafés, and the ballet. Rather than completing staged portraits, Degas captured his dancers in the midst of movement and highlighted their athleticism through unexpected vantage points. This is one of more than 1,500 works Degas produced on the subject, but it is unusual in its depiction of ruins on the hilltop in the background.

Scene with Ballerinas

COQ AU VIN

Liz Grenamyer **CATERING BY LIZ GRENAMYER**

Serves 4

1 *cup* chopped raw bacon
2 chicken breasts, skin on,
   airline breast, if possible
2 chicken thighs, skin on
2 chicken legs, skin on
2 *cups* all-purpose flour, for dredging
2 *cups* diced carrots
2 *cups* baby bella mushrooms, sliced
8 *cloves* garlic, minced
1 *cup* diced celery
2 *cups* pearl onions, peeled
2 *cups* red wine
1 ½ *quarts* chicken broth
Bouquet garni with 3 *sprigs* thyme and
   2 *sprigs* rosemary
2 bay leaves
2 *cups* Yukon potatoes, peeled, medium dice
2 *tablespoons* kosher salt
1 *tablespoon* black pepper

Preheat oven to 375 degrees.

Cook bacon in a pan over medium heat until fat renders out.

Meanwhile, season chicken with salt and pepper and dredge both sides in flour.

Remove bacon from pan with a slotted spoon. Sear chicken in bacon fat until golden brown on both sides, working in batches as necessary. Remove chicken from pan with tongs and place on rack.

Add carrots, mushrooms, garlic, celery, and pearl onions to bacon fat and chicken renderings; stir to coat. Deglaze pan with red wine, scraping bits of seared chicken from bottom of pan with a wooden spoon. Cook until wine is reduced by a third.

Add chicken broth, bouquet garni, bay leaves, and potatoes to pan. Bring back to a simmer. Add chicken back to pan, skin side up, and cover with a tight-fitting lid.

Roast for 50 minutes or until internal temperature of chicken reaches 165 degrees.

"

I've always fallen for Degas paintings because of the fabulous light. I envision him with fellow artists in the Saint Germain district of Paris sharing a meal at one of the many brasseries and bistros. Coq au vin is a very traditional and iconic dish found in these eateries of Paris and typifies what 'starving' artists might enjoy.

—Liz Grenamyer
Scene with Ballerinas

"

Pago Pago *inspired me to create a tropical recipe that draws inspiration from the post-war cocktail culture. The classic, sepia-toned look of the artwork gives a warm and tropical feel to the piece and I can almost hear lap steel guitar music playing over the radios as waves crash on the shore beyond the porch. The man in uniform looks relaxed after a day at work and what better way to relax with than a cocktail? Alcoholic or not. With this in mind we created a Coffee Painkiller Tiki. The Painkiller is a classic rum-based tiki drink. In this recipe, we've subbed out the rum for coffee and rum syrup while creating a creamy balance with coconut milk highlighted by pineapple juice, bitters, and freshly grated nutmeg.*

—*Zack Burnett*
Pago Pago

Pago Pago

COFFEE PAINKILLER TIKI

Zack Burnett **BOLD BEAN COFFEE ROASTERS**

Makes 1 cocktail

4 ounces cold brewed Bold Bean Sweet Spot Blend
2 ounces coconut milk
2 ounces pineapple juice
1 ounce rum syrup
8 dashes Angostura bitters
Freshly grated nutmeg
Maraschino cherry

Mix coffee, coconut milk, pineapple juice, rum syrup, and bitters in a cocktail shaker with cubed ice. Shake until cocktail shaker is frosty. Strain into a tiki mug full of crushed ice. Grate nutmeg over drink, then garnish with one maraschino cherry and an umbrella.

RUM SYRUP

1 cup dark rum
1 cup white sugar
1 ¼ cups water

Combine ingredients in a medium saucepan and bring to a boil. Lower heat and simmer for 10 minutes. Let cool before using.

Whitfield Lovell
American, b. 1959
Pago Pago
2008
Conté on wood with radios and sound
Purchased with funds from the Morton R. Hirschberg Bequest and funds provided by the Jacksonville Community
AP.2015.2.1

Lauded for his detailed portraits of anonymous African Americans, Whitfield Lovell invents histories for the unknown faces he finds in period photographs. Named for the capital of American Samoa, Pago Pago depicts a soldier in a World War II uniform. In a period where African Americans had limited prospects, the military offered opportunities that civilian life did not. This soldier, reclining in a bamboo chair, appears confident despite the inherent risks of military service. Lovell juxtaposed this image with period Bakelite radios that conceal modern-day speakers, allowing Billie Holiday's I Cover the Waterfront to resonate seamlessly from the piece, and transport the viewer into another era.

Parade to War, Allegory

SEARED RED GROUPER, LEMONGRASS-SCENTED BROTH, FLAGEOLET BEANS, BABY CARROTS, FENNEL, PICKLED WATERMELON RADISH, AND LEMON AND TARRAGON OILS

Ian Lynch **BISTRO AIX**

Serves 2

Red grouper filets
1 tablespoon canola oil
1 tablespoon unsalted butter
1 pound clams
Fish Stock
Flageolet Beans
Baby Carrots
Roasted Fennel
Upland cress, fennel fronds, micro sango
  radish and micro basil, to garnish
Pickled Watermelon Radish
Lemon Oil
Tarragon Herb Oil
Salt and freshly ground black pepper

Preheat oven to 375 degrees.

Pat fish dry with a paper towel and season with salt and pepper. Add oil to a medium sauté pan and heat over medium-high heat until almost smoking. Gently place fish in pan and sear until golden brown, around 3 to 5 minutes.

Turn fish over and sear the other side until golden brown. Remove fish and place in an oven-safe pan with butter, then bake until just cooked through. Exact cooking time will depend on the size of the fish, so check it often.

While the fish is baking, heat flageolet beans in a little of their cooking liquid and season to taste. Steam clams in fish stock.

Using a slotted spoon, place beans in the center of a large shallow bowl, then place roasted baby carrots across beans. Place two pieces of roasted fennel next to the beans, then gently ladle about a cup of fish broth into the bowl. Place seared fish on top of beans and baby carrots. Arrange upland cress, micro sango radish, fennel fronds, and micro basil around the fish. Place pickled watermelon radish on top of fish then finish with a few drops of lemon and tarragon oil.

FISH STOCK

2 tablespoons olive oil
1 large leek, chopped
3 ribs celery, chopped
2 bulbs fennel, chopped
4 cloves garlic, smashed
2 cups white wine
1 pound white fish bones
Lemongrass
1 bay leaf
1 teaspoon pink peppercorns
1 teaspoon green peppercorns
8 cups water

Heat oil in a large saucepan over medium heat until hot but not smoking. Add leek, celery, fennel, and garlic, and sauté until translucent, about 8 minutes.

Deglaze with white wine and simmer for 6 to 8 minutes. Add fish bones, lemongrass, bay leaf, pink and green peppercorns, and water. Bring to a simmer and cook for about 30 minutes until aromatic.

Strain stock through a fine mesh sieve and skim off any fat.

FLAGEOLET BEANS

½ cup flageolet beans, soaked overnight
½ carrot, chopped
1 rib celery, chopped
¼ yellow onion, chopped

Place all ingredients in a medium saucepan and cover with water.

Simmer over medium heat until beans are tender, about 30-45 minutes. Drain beans and reserve cooking liquid.

BABY CARROTS

3 baby carrots
1 knob butter

Blanch baby carrots in boiling salted water for 2 minutes. Once finished, immediately transfer to an ice bath to stop the cooking process.

When ready to plate, heat carrots in a sauté pan with butter and season to taste with salt and pepper.

ROASTED FENNEL

1 bulb fennel, cored (reserve fronds for garnish)
¼ cup olive oil
¼ cup water
Salt and pepper, to taste

Preheat oven to 350 degrees.

Cut fennel in half lengthwise, then cut crosswise into ¼ inch slices.

Place fennel in a baking dish. Cover with olive oil and water. Bake for 25 minutes and season with salt and pepper.

TARRAGON HERB OIL

1 cup chives
1 cup tarragon
1 cup flat leaf parsley
1 cup canola oil

Blanch the chives, tarragon, and flat leaf parsley in boiling salted water for 20 seconds and immediately shock in ice water to stop the cooking process.

Remove herbs from water and squeeze out any excess liquid. Roughly chop the herbs and place in a blender with the oil. Puree for 3 minutes; the herbs should be bright green.

Strain oil through a fine mesh sieve and transfer to a squeeze bottle.

PICKLED WATERMELON RADISH

1 carrot, peeled
1 tablespoon salt
1 bay leaf
1 watermelon radish, peeled and thinly sliced
1 ½ cups seasoned rice wine vinegar
½ cup water
1 teaspoon black peppercorns
1 serrano chili pepper, halved

Peel carrot into thin ribbons using a vegetable peeler. Place ribbons in a bowl and toss with salt, bay leaf, and watermelon radish.

In medium saucepan, boil the vinegar, water, peppercorns, and chili pepper. Remove from heat and cool slightly, then pour over carrot mixture.

LEMON OIL

1 large lemon, washed and dried
1 cup olive oil

Remove the zest from the lemon, avoiding the bitter white pith. Place the lemon zest and olive oil in a small sauce pan and warm over medium heat—do not let the oil simmer. Cook for about 10 minutes, then remove from heat and allow to cool.

John Steuart Curry
American, 1897 – 1946
Parade to War, Allegory
1938
Oil on canvas
Gift of Barnett Banks, Inc.
AG.1991.4.1

Painted in the years between the Great Depression and World War II, Parade to War, Allegory *reflects many Americans' apprehension about joining the looming conflict. John Steuart Curry transformed a celebratory parade into a gruesome scene, where young soldiers morph into skeletons. Beneath the streamers and waving flags, Curry portrays conflicting emotions. In the center of the canvas, a young woman in a white dress and two small boys seem unaware of the impending peril, while two women in the foreground are distraught and overcome with grief.*

This painting was completed after the Great Depression, a time when people turned to growing their own gardens to provide food for their families. I wanted to create a dish that reflects that same garden-to-table mentality. My dish incorporates regionally-grown ingredients and a locally-caught red grouper.

One of my biggest sources of inspiration as chef is my wife and family. When I looked at this painting, I saw a beautiful woman walking next to a soldier and playing children, and was instantly reminded of my family. The faces on each soldier reflect how their fates have all been predetermined by the war. When I leave for work, I am always thinking about my family and how important they are in my life.

—Ian Lynch
Parade to War, Allegory

Alessandro Gherardini
Italian, 1655 – 1723
The Forge of Vulcan
c. 1688 – 1689
Oil on canvas
Gift of Mr. and Mrs. Kendrick Guernsey
AG.1972.15.1

*Florentine painter Alessandro Gherardini received many
commissions to decorate church interiors as well as private
villas. In this painting, he recreated a scene from Virgil's
Aenid. Venus, mother of the hero Aeneas, implored her
husband, Vulcan, the god of fire, to make a shield to
protect her son. Here, Vulcan's Cyclopes labor over
the molten metal.*

66

I was drawn to The Forge of Vulcan *because the brightest spot in the painting is the light radiating from the fire. The warm red and gold tones combined with the bright white light in the center of the painting remind me of cooking in Ovinté's kitchen. From my perspective, the "brightest spot" in the restaurant is the kitchen because of all the activity and energy. My dish is a traditional Italian porterhouse and was finished in a wood-fired oven. Gherardini's work really captures the challenges that arise when working with fire, and I wanted my dish to be something that involved working with fire. I also wanted my dish to reflect the same amount of warmth and brightness that you see when you look at Gherardini's work. I was inspired by the amount of teamwork that is shown in this painting. Gherardini's piece reminded me of all the hard work that goes on in the kitchen.*

—Ian Lynch
The Forge of Vulcan

The Forge of Vulcan

BISTECCA ALLA FIORENTINA

Ian Lynch **OVINTE**

MUSHROOMS

3 royal trumpet mushrooms
½ *cup* brown beech mushrooms
½ *cup* nebrodini mushrooms
1 *tablespoon* canola oil
1 *tablespoon* butter
Salt and pepper

Clean any dirt from the mushrooms. Cut the ends off all of the mushrooms, split the royal trumpets in half, and break up the brown beech mushrooms.

Heat 1 tablespoon canola oil in a large sauté pan. Sauté royal trumpet and nebrodini mushrooms together for 2 minutes, then add the brown beech. Add 1 tablespoon butter and season with salt and pepper. Set mushrooms aside.

GARLIC CONFIT

1 *head* of garlic
Extra virgin olive oil

Preheat oven to 200 degrees.

Place head of garlic in a small baking dish and cover with olive oil. Cover tightly with foil and bake for about 30 minutes until garlic is tender. Squeeze garlic out of skins and reserve.

CIPOLLINI ONIONS

6 cipollini onions
2 *tablespoons* olive oil

Remove ends and skin from onions. Place in a small baking dish and cover with 2 tablespoons of olive oil and ¼ cup of water. Wrap with foil and place in a 200 degree oven for 45 minutes to one hour, or until tender.

RAPINI AND FAVA BEANS

1 *cup* fava beans, shelled
1 *bunch* rapini, ends removed

Fill a medium-sized saucepan ¾ full of water. Heavily salt water and bring to a boil. Boil fava beans for 90 seconds, then remove and immediately place in an ice bath. Remove skins from beans.

Blanch rapini in the same water for 2 minutes and remove to ice bath.

PORTERHOUSE

2 ½ *pound* porterhouse steak
Olive oil
2 *tablespoons* chopped rosemary
1 lemon, cut in half and grilled
Sea salt and freshly ground black pepper

Preheat oven to 450 degrees.

Let steak rest at room temperature for 30 minutes before cooking.

Generously season steak with salt, pepper, olive oil, and half the rosemary. Grill or sear steak in a cast iron pan on each side for 5 to 6 minutes. Place in oven if needed to bring to desired temperature. Allow steak to rest for 5 minutes before serving.

To serve, sauté blanched rapini in a little canola oil and unsalted butter. Season with salt and pepper.

Place rapini on a large platter. Add sautéed mushrooms, cipolini onions, garlic confit, and fava beans around the platter.

Place steak on top of vegetables and drizzle with olive oil. Finish with chopped rosemary and lemon juice from the grilled lemons.

Perugia

HONEY MUSTARD PORK OSSO BUCCO WITH CREAMED HOMINY, PICKLED MUSTARD GREENS WITH CARROT TOPS, ROASTED CARROTS, AND SUNCHOKE CHIPS

Margie Ashens **NORTH BEACH FISH CAMP**

Serves 4

CREAMED HOMINY

4 cups fresh or frozen hominy
1 cup heavy cream
8 tablespoons butter
Salt and pepper

Rinse hominy and place in a large pot. Cover completely with water and add salt.

Bring to a boil then reduce heat and simmer approximately 3 hours or until tender, adding water as needed. Drain hominy then place back on heat with cream and butter. Simmer over low heat until hominy achieves a thick creamy texture, then season with salt and pepper to taste.

PICKLED MUSTARD GREENS WITH CARROT TOPS

2 cups water
¼ cup rice wine vinegar
1 tablespoon salt
2 tablespoons sugar
2 tablespoons diced shallot
1 teaspoon chopped garlic
2 serrano chiles, split
Pepper, to taste
½ pound mustard greens, cleaned and chopped
Reserved carrot tops from roasted carrots

Bring all ingredients except greens to a boil. Simmer 5 minutes to infuse flavor. Remove from heat and cool slightly.

Pour liquid over mustard greens and carrot tops. Cover and place in refrigerator.

PORK OSSO BUCCO

4 - 12 ounce to 1 pound pork shanks
Olive oil
4 ounces Nueske's bacon, cut into strips
1 cup medium diced leek, onion, carrot, and celery
3 teaspoons chopped garlic
½ pound crimini mushrooms
1 sprig each of rosemary, thyme, bay leaf
1 cup dark ale
1 ½ cups chicken stock
1 ½ cups veal stock
½ cup whole grain mustard
½ cup local honey
1 bunch of carrots, roasted, green tops reserved
Salt and pepper
Sunchoke chips, for garnish

Preheat oven to 325 degrees.

Season pork shanks with salt and pepper. Heat olive oil in a large pan over medium-high heat and sear pork on all sides until brown. Remove pork from pan and pour off excess oil.

Place bacon in the same pan and cook to render out fat. Add vegetables, garlic, mushrooms, and herbs. Cook until softened, then add dark ale. Bring to a simmer for about 3 minutes. Add chicken stock, veal stock, mustard, and honey. Bring to a boil, taste, and adjust seasonings as needed.

Place pork shank in a roasting dish and pour hot broth over pork. Cover and bake for 1 ½ to 2 hours, until pork is tender but not falling off bone.

When meat is tender, remove from liquid and keep warm. Strain liquid through a fine mesh strainer into a saucepot and reduce over medium-high heat until thickened. Taste sauce and re-adjust seasonings.

To serve:

Place creamed hominy in the center of a plate. Surround with roasted carrots and top with pork osso bucco and a generous drizzle of sauce. Top with pickled greens and sunchoke chips.

George Inness
American, 1825 – 1894
Perugia
1870
Oil on canvas
Bequest of Ninah M. H. Cummer
C.0.195.1

A seminal figure in the development of American landscape painting, George Inness lived in Italy from 1870 until 1874, specifically to create travel scenes for Boston art dealers Williams and Everett. Inness completed nearly 200 paintings that represented everyday life and popular attractions, in addition to more generic landscapes. In Perugia, Inness captured an Italian peasant in the countryside near the ancient Etruscan town of the same name. Inness' travel abroad exposed him to the works of his European contemporaries in the Romantic and Barbizon traditions, which influenced his soft and poetic canvases.

66

Memory is defined as the process of recalling what has been learned and retained. What Inness has inspired for me in his painting Perugia *is a collection of memories, old and new, revolving around amazing vacations and of course—food!*

From Italy I borrowed osso buco, replacing the beloved veal with pork, but with respect to some of its classic elements and my love for the deeply flavored cuisine for which Italy is famous. Using a braising technique is a nod to my parents' Sunday suppers (thanks mom and dad!) for I believe that, when a family prepares a meal and eats together, great things happen. It is a tradition that still continues.

I incorporated a Southern influence with creamed hominy (thanks Ben!) and pickled mustard greens to represent a new chapter where I am working with talented people, learning every day, and looking forward to creating the next memory.

—Margie Ashens
Perugia

Camille Pissarro
French, 1830 – 1903
Les Glaneuses (The Gleaners)
c. 1889
Gouache with charcoal, crayon and
watercolor on paper
Purchased with funds from the
Morton R. Hirschberg Bequest
AP.2004.3.1

In 1884, Camille Pissarro and his family left Paris for the small hamlet of Éragny-sur-Epte. In Les Glaneuses, he recorded women in the field capturing meager remains after the harvest. This laborious work was done by the rural poor, who were allowed to keep whatever grain they could salvage. Beginning in the 1870s, Pissarro embarked on a series of images that celebrated this menial task, and he depicted the workers with dignity. This gouache, a heavy, opaque watercolor, is a preparatory work for an oil painting of the same name in the collection of the Kunstmuseum in Basel, Switzerland.

Les Glaneuses
(The Gleaners)

BELGIAN PALE ALE

Pale Ale 5.5% ABV | 25 IBU
AARDWOLF

Aardwolf Belgian Pale Ale is a malt-forward, sessionable ale. Brewed with traditional European hops and malts, it is then fermented using a carefully selected Belgian yeast strain, thus imparting a unique spicy and fruity character.

The Belgian Pale has been around since the conception of Aardwolf and was originally viewed as a way to continually cultivate and keep a Belgian yeast strain in-house to help us increase the variety of beer we could brew. It has since become our most popular offering in both the tap room and through distribution. Our Belgian Pale is a perfect mix of both flavor and drinkability. This pale ale features a unique flavor profile for everyone from the craft novice to the most discerning of palettes.

DUKES COLD NOSE BROWN ALE

5% ABV | 23 IBU
BOLD CITY BREWERY

A mild brown ale named after Duke, the owner's late beloved boxer. This local favorite has hints of chocolate and caramel with a smooth nutty finish. A well balanced, flavorful brown ale that is perfect for any time of year.

Dukes Cold Nose Brown Ale was first brewed in 2009 and is very meaningful to the Miller family. Duke, the owner's late beloved boxer, was diagnosed with kidney disease and Brian wanted to brew a beer for Duke because he was such a big part of the brewery and his family. We never thought Dukes Cold Nose Brown Ale would become the brand it is.

ROUTE 90 RYE

6% ABV | 60 IBU
ENGINE 15 BREWING CO.

This beer is a twist on the venerable Pale Ale style. We use 11% rye malt in the mash to create a spicy note that is distinct and different from that lent by hops. The addition of rye also tends to dry out the finish. Route 90 Rye is rich in malt flavor but balanced with generous additions of American and German hops added late in the boil, which lend their piney and earthy notes to round out this complex beer. This beer complements spicy food very well, but is quite flexible and pairs well with rich foods such as earthy cheeses and hearty meat dishes.

Route 90 Rye was the first beer we brewed commercially at Engine 15 Brewing Co. We initially ran a naming contest and for some years it was known by another name. We actually had to change the name 3 years in when we found out that another brewery had the trademark! We thought long and hard about what the new name should be. In 2013 we acquired a historic property that would become our production brewery and decided on Route 90 Rye as a nod to the avenue in Jacksonville that connects our two breweries, which lie almost 30 miles apart. Route 90 is one of our flagship beers and has won many awards including Runner up - Best Beer in Florida in 2014.

DOUBLE OVERHEAD DOUBLE IPA

9.1% ABV | 80 IBU
GREEN ROOM BREWING

Double Overhead is brewed with all Columbus hops and then dry-hopped with Columbus and whole leaf Cascade. This produces a complex, resinousy hop aroma and signature over-the-top hop bitterness that make it a favorite in our tap room. The double IPA boasts a piney-grapefruit taste and is well-balanced and drinkable, especially for a beer with this ABV.

We started brewing Double Overhead as soon as we opened. We knew early on that we wanted to keep a double IPA on tap year-round because most breweries at the time only rolled one out seasonally. The beer is named after a wave that surfers always talk about, but we rarely see in Florida. A special hurricane might bring double overhead waves but they tend to be elusive and something you have to travel to find. This double IPA is a challenging, yet rewarding experience, just like the wave it's named after.

HONEY BADGER IMPERIAL BELGIAN-STYLE FARMHOUSE SAISON

8.5% ABV | 35 IBU
INTUITION ALE WORKS

Traditionally, Belgian saisons are low alcohol, sessionable beers. Honey Badger respects the Belgian style by using a simple grain bill and traditional yeast but does its own thing with local honey for an added kick.

We started brewing Honey Badger in the summer of 2011 and it is one of the first specialty saisons that we brewed here at Intuition Ale Works. We were attracted to this style for a number of reasons. First of all, we enjoy and have a great respect for Belgian beers. It was only natural to try our hand and add our own twist to one of the Belgian styles that is perfectly fitting for hot Southern summers. Honey Badger also provided us with an early opportunity to incorporate local ingredients. We source the honey locally for each batch and we don't always get the same variety of honey so there are subtle changes to the flavor and aroma.

IMPERIAL RED ALE

7.8% ABV | 25 IBU
PINGLEHEAD BREWING COMPANY

Pinglehead's flagship beer pours a clear red body with an off-white colored head. Aroma is caramel sweet with floral undertones. Dry-hopping gives subtle floral hop aromas to complement a smooth caramel malt backbone. A combination of mellow bitterness, candy sweetness, and medium body result in a balanced, highly drinkable red ale.

Pinglehead Brewing Company has set out to produce unapologetic beer in styles that will translate to a very specific crowd of beer lovers. Beer lovers who would not need to be spoon-fed warning labels, enjoy dates, or given the impression that Pinglehead uses a process unlike anyone else. The Imperial Red was brewed as a prime example that a beer can be assertive and still be considered balanced and drinkable for the masses.

SCOUT DOG 44
GERMAN-STYLE AMBER ALE
(ALT BIER)

5.4% ABV | 30 IBU
VETERANS UNITED CRAFT BREWERY

Scout Dog 44 unleashes flavor with a rich biscuit and light caramel malt backbone perfectly balanced with noble hop bitterness. Stand above the pack and savor this easy-drinking amber.

The name, Scout Dog 44, was inspired by a friend of the brewery, John Burnam. John was a Dog Handler from the 44th Infantry Platoon during the Vietnam War. Following a successful military career, John led the initiative to recognize military working dogs and their handlers by helping to establish the Military Working Dog Teams National Monument.

To honor and help raise awareness of the invaluable service of our 4-footed warriors, Veterans United was proud to name one of our favorite beers after these silent heroes. As a near and dear cause to the brewery's founders, Veterans United is working with several canine organizations to help increase attention and raise funds for their initiatives; organizations to date include Military Working Dog Team Support Association and Florida Service Dogs.

RUBY BEACH
WHEAT ALE
6% ABV | 15 IBU

ZETA BREWING COMPANY

Ruby Beach is an unfiltered American Wheat Ale brewed with Florida orange and finished with fresh raspberries. Naturally occurring lactic acid from the acidulated malt adds balance and helps bring out the tartness of the raspberries.

Ruby Beach, one of our first core brands, was inspired by the city of Ruby Beach, the original name of Jacksonville Beach when it was founded in 1884. This bright, crisp, and refreshing beer reflects our location in the heart of Jax Beach just steps away from the ocean.

66

Early 20th-century Paris is easily one of the most intriguing and inspiring

periods in history to me. The café scene Miller painted perfectly embodies

all the opulence and glamour of pre-war Paris: civility and elegance the

overwhelming theme on the inside, while I imagine the streets outside abuzz

with a more "la boheme" philosophy, courtesy of the influx of artists residing

in Montmartre. The clash of traditional and unorthodox has been prevalent

though out my life, and perfectly embodies what I aimed to achieve in this

dish. Miller's love for Paris is undeniable in this piece. I wanted to mirror

that adoration with an indulgent dessert highlighting a few of my favorite

French-sourced ingredients, while being mindful of color and composition.

The unconventional comes into play in an otherwise traditional-looking tart

by way of ingredients. A tart sans butter? I hope the French can forgive me

for my radical ways.

—Katie Riehm
Café L'Avenue, Paris

Café L'Avenue, Paris

ESPRESSO CHOCOLATE TART WITH ST. GERMAINE-MACERATED BERRIES,
BOURBON VANILLA BEAN COCONUT CREAM, LAVENDER CARAMEL, AND FLEUR DE SEL

Katie Riehm **SWEET THEORY BAKING CO.**

Serves 10 – 12

MACERATED BERRIES

3 cups mixed berries
3 tablespoons granulated sugar
Juice of half a lemon
⅓ cup St. Germaine elderflower liqueur

Gently toss all ingredients in a large bowl. Refrigerate for at least 6 hours or overnight.

TART SHELL

2 cups Bob's Red Mill all-purpose gluten-free flour
½ cup sweet white rice flour
1 teaspoon xanthan gum
⅓ cup confectioner's sugar, sifted
½ teaspoon sea salt
1 vanilla bean, halved, seeds scrapped
8 tablespoons coconut oil

Preheat oven to 350 degrees.

In a medium bowl, sift together flours and xanthan gum. In another medium bowl, combine confectioner's sugar, salt, vanilla bean seeds, and coconut oil. Add the flour mixture to the oil mixture in two batches, until a soft dough forms.

Drop the dough into a 10-inch tart pan with a removable bottom and carefully press into the pan, trying to keep the dough as thin and evenly distributed as possible, particularly around the scalloped edges. Shave off any excess dough with a knife. Cover the pan and refrigerate for 10 to 15 minutes.

Once chilled, prick the shell with a fork all around the bottom and bake for 16 to 20 minutes until golden brown. Remove from the oven and allow to cool while you prepare the filling.

ESPRESSO CHOCOLATE FILLING

2 cans full fat coconut milk
10 ounces bittersweet chocolate
3 tablespoons coconut oil
⅓ cup agave nectar
2 tablespoons espresso
⅛ teaspoon sea salt
½ teaspoon fleur de sel, for garnish

Scrape the thick, white cream layer off the top of the two cans of coconut (Do not shake your coconut milk cans!), leaving the liquid behind. Set aside.

In a double boiler, melt the chocolate until completely smooth. Remove from the heat and stir in coconut cream, coconut oil, agave nectar, espresso, and sea salt. Pour into cooled tart shell, and refrigerate for at least 4 hours until completely set. Keep refrigerated until ready to serve.

LAVENDER CARAMEL

¾ cup granulated sugar
¼ cup water
¼ cup agave nectar
1 ½ teaspoons lavender
2 tablespoons soy free Earth Balance butter
½ cup plain coconut creamer
¼ teaspoon sea salt

In a medium saucepan on medium-high heat, combine the sugar, water, and agave nectar. Heat until the sugar dissolves, then increase heat to high to bring the mixture to a boil. Boil until caramel is a medium amber brown color, around 5 to 7 minutes.

Remove from heat and add in lavender, Earth Balance, and coconut creamer, whisking quickly to combine. Allow caramel to sit for 15 minutes, then strain out the lavender buds.

BOURBON VANILLA BEAN COCONUT CREAM

2 cans full fat coconut milk, chilled
⅓ cup confectioner's sugar, sifted
1 vanilla bean, halved, seeds scraped

Place cans of coconut milk in the refrigerator 6 hours or overnight to chill. Once cold, scrape off the top, thickened cream, leaving the liquid behind.

In a chilled metal bowl, beat together the coconut cream, sugar, and vanilla bean seeds with a hand mixer until light and fluffy, about 3 minutes. Keep refrigerated until ready to serve.

To serve:

Remove tart from refrigerator and garnish with fleur de sel. Carefully portion out and cut the tart, serving it with the macerated berries, bourbon vanilla coconut cream, and lavender caramel.

Richard Emile Miller
American, 1875 – 1943
Café L'Avenue, Paris
c. 1906 – 1910
Oil on canvas
Purchased with funds
from the Cummer Council
AP.1985.1.1

American Richard Emile Miller was part of a group of expatriate artists who settled in the French village of Giverny to be near renowned Impressionist Claude Monet (1840 – 1926). Although the Impressionistic style of quick brushstrokes that captured an "impression" of reality failed to resonate with American artists or consumers initially, eventually it became popular as a "modern" way to represent life. Here, Miller captured a lively French café, where fashionable women listen to a trio of musicians. His ebullient brushstrokes mimic the energy of the participants, as onlookers peer in from the street-side windows.

Crucifixion in Yellow

MANGO BLACK BEAN SALSA WITH AVOCADO AND CHARRED CORN

Debbie and Don Nicol **TACOLU**

Serves 8 – 10

1 ripe mango, peeled and diced
1 – 15 ounce can black beans, drained and rinsed
1 bunch cilantro, chopped
1 large lime, juiced
1 jalapeño, seeded and diced
2 red sweet peppers, seeded and chopped
1 cup roasted and charred corn kernels
1 tablespoon coarsely diced red onion
1 ripe large avocado, diced
Salt and pepper, to taste

Mix all ingredients except avocado in a large bowl. Gently fold avocado into the salsa and season to taste with salt and pepper.

Enjoy on a taco with any meat of your choice or alone with fresh tortilla chips.

Best if eaten immediately after making, but will hold in the refrigerator for a few days.

PREVIOUS PAGE:

Abraham Rattner
American, 1895 – 1978
Crucifixion in Yellow
1953
Oil on Masonite
Gift of Genny, Clifford, and Robert Ayers
in memory of Genevieve Schultz Ayers
AG.1987.7.1

After serving in World War I, Abraham Rattner, the American-born son of a Russian rabbi, returned to Paris on a fellowship to study art. He remained there for nearly 20 years, and became heavily influenced by both contemporary abstract trends as well as more historic styles. His simplified forms, especially those later in his career, recall Romanesque and Medieval traditions. In this painting, Rattner combined bright jewel tones with thick black outlines, like the stained glass windows he admired at the cathedral in Chartres, France.

Courtesy of SPC Foundation, Inc. and Leepa-Rattner Museum of Art

We were inspired by the bold colors and textures of this painting by Abraham Rattner, just as we are by the colors, textures, and flavors of Mexican cuisine. In the same way Rattner shatters and reassembles the image of a figure on a golden cross for Crucifixion in Yellow, *cooking is often the process of shattering, or breaking down ingredients and reassembling them into something new. Common ingredients are sliced, diced, macerated, marinated, manipulated into what is an entirely different, but (hopefully) harmonious piece. How those ingredients are combined, seasoned, and reproduced as a new dish is the true art of cooking.*

—Debbie and Don Nicol
Crucifixion in Yellow

Ecuelle and Stand

DECONSTRUCTED QUAIL BOURGUIGNON "POT-AU-FEU"

Toben Stubee **5LOAVES 2FISH MOBILE KITCHEN FOOD TRUCK**

Serves 2

QUAIL

2 semi-boneless quail, butterflied
4 tablespoons butter, divided
4 sprigs thyme
2 tablespoons chopped garlic
3 tablespoons red wine
1 cup roasted poultry stock

Season quail with salt and pepper. Melt 3 tablespoons butter in a saute pan over medium-high heat and add quail, thyme sprigs, and garlic. Baste quail with butter until golden brown, crisp, and cooked through. Remove quail from pan and set aside.

Deglaze pan with red wine, then add poultry stock and reduce liquid by a quarter. Remove sauce from heat and whisk in remaining 1 tablespoon butter.

YELLOW BEET PUREE

1 yellow gold beet, peeled
2 cups chicken stock
1 tablespoon turmeric
Salt and pepper
Splash apple cider vinegar

Boil the yellow beet in chicken stock until tender. Remove from stock and puree in blender with turmeric, salt, pepper, and a splash of cider vinegar.

YELLOW BEET CHIPS

Canola oil, for frying
1 yellow gold beet, peeled and thinly sliced
Salt and pepper

Heat canola oil to 300 degrees. Fry beet chips until crispy. Season with salt and pepper.

ROASTED RED BEETS

1 red beet
1 sprig thyme
1 clove garlic
1 tablespoon olive oil
Salt and pepper

Preheat oven to 350 degrees.

Place all ingredients in a roasting dish and cover with foil. Roast for 30 minutes, until beet is tender. Peel and dice beet, then combine with roasting juices that accumulated in pan.

BABY CARROTS

6 baby carrots
1 tablespoon butter, melted
Salt and pepper

Blanch carrots in boiling salted water until softened. Drain, then toss with melted butter, salt, and pepper.

GOLD POTATOES

6 small gold potatoes
4 cups chicken stock

Boil potatoes in chicken stock until tender. Remove and season with salt and pepper.

FOIE GRAS MOUSSE

2 ounces foie gras
¼ cup heavy cream
Salt and pepper
4 slices baguette, toasted

Heat a heavy-bottomed pan over high heat. Sear foie gras until cooked through. Remove to a plate and allow to cool, then puree in a blender until smooth.

Whisk heavy cream in a bowl until stiff. Fold foie gras puree into whipped cream. Season with salt and pepper and spread onto baguettes.

Meissen Porcelain Manufactory
German, 1710
Ecuelle and Stand
c. 1740
Porcelain
Gift of Miss Constance I. and Ralph H. Wark
AG.2000.2.147

This ecuelle (a small covered bowl for soup) and stand reveal the scope of the Meissen Manufactory's design work. In the middle years of the 18th century, illustrators shifted from fanciful depictions of life in China to motifs that reflected Europe's interest in the natural sciences, particularly the investigation and classification of animals. Here, the artist combined images of a turkey with European songbirds and insects.

"

Many pieces in the Wark Collection of Early Meissen Porcelain feature stylized European landscapes, which is where I drew my inspiration. French cuisine at the time was coming into what we know today as "Haute" cuisine, or "High Cooking." Multiple-course place settings were commonplace.

My dish is a contemporary interpretation of the classic French Pot-au-feu, which was the quintessential French dish in the mid-1700s, the time when the Ecuelle and Stand was made and possibly even used for the dish. Classically, it is a beef stew, where the bone marrow was served as a first course, followed by the broth (which may have been served in a vessel like this), then the meat and vegetables. The plate combines the three courses into one.

At the same time, and before the time when Escoffier codified French cooking, sauces like coulis and rich brown meat stocks were also commonplace. I drew upon those ideas to come up with a dish that incorporated concepts of the three courses, along with color cues and visual depictions for my final interpretation. The main ideas I drew were yellow tones, fowl, a wine barrel, and a cup used for broth or soup.

—Toben Stubee
Ecuelle and Stand

Nightfall at the Hangar

GRILLED VEAL CHOP WITH POTATO DAUPHINOISE,
PORTOBELLO MUSHROOMS, AND RED WINE MUSHROOM GLAZE

David Medure **RESTAURANT MEDURE**

Serves 4

POTATO DAUPHINOISE

Butter
1 large onion, thinly sliced
1 tablespoon chopped garlic
2 eggs
4 ounces boursin cheese
Juice of 1 lemon
2 cups heavy cream
4 Idaho potatoes, thinly sliced
1 tablespoon unsalted butter, sliced
½ cup breadcrumbs
Olive oil

Preheat oven to 400 degrees and butter a baking dish.

Caramelize onion and garlic in butter in a saute pan, then chill for a few minutes in refrigerator.

Meanwhile, whisk eggs, boursin, lemon juice, and heavy cream in a medium mixing bowl. Add potatoes, caramelized onions, and garlic, then using your hands, mix all ingredients together until potatoes are heavily coated.

Place potatoes in buttered baking dish, then lay butter slices over top of the mixture. Cover with aluminum foil or a baking dish lid and bake for 45 minutes.

Evenly distribute breadcrumbs on top of potatoes, drizzle with oil, and bake for another 10 minutes, or until breadcrumbs are golden brown. Allow potatoes to rest for 10 minutes before serving.

GRILLED VEAL CHOP

4 bone-in veal chops
Olive oil
Salt and pepper

Coat veal chops with olive oil, salt, and pepper, then let rest at room temperature for 20 minutes before grilling.

Grill both sides of veal chops until golden brown. Depending on the size of the veal chops and desired temperature, you may need to finish veal in the oven at 400 degrees. Remember to leave meat slightly under desired temperature to allow for broiling the gratin.

PORTOBELLO AND BLUE CHEESE GRATIN

3 portobello mushroom caps
Olive oil
Salt and pepper
Bleu cheese, as needed

Preheat oven to 400 degrees.

Heavily coat three portobello caps with olive oil and season with salt and pepper. Place mushrooms in a baking dish, cover, and bake for 20 minutes. Allow mushrooms to cool then cut into medium size pieces.

Increase oven temperature to broil.

Place a large spoonful of mushrooms and desired amount of blue cheese on top of veal chops. Place veal on the top rack and broil until cheese begins to melt, 1 to 2 minutes.

MUSHROOM SAUCE

8 shiitake mushrooms, sliced
2 shallots, sliced
1 tablespoon chopped garlic
½ cup red wine
2 quarts beef stock
1 tablespoon unsalted butter, cold
1 teaspoon chopped fresh thyme
2 tablespoons cold butter
Salt and pepper

Season mushrooms with salt and pepper, and sauté on medium-heat until tender. Add shallots and garlic. Cook for a few minutes then deglaze with red wine. Let the wine cook down until it is almost dry. Add beef stock and fresh thyme to pan and simmer for 20 minutes. Whisk in cold butter and season to taste.

Serve veal chops with potato dauphinoise, mushroom sauce, and steamed haricot verts.

Philip Evergood
American, 1901 – 1973
Nightfall at the Hangar
1937
Oil on canvas
Purchased with funds from the
Morton R. Hirschberg Bequest
AP. 2007.1.1

Philip Evergood considered himself a social realist painter and dedicated his career to representing scenes of contemporary life. With their harsh colors and exaggerated, cartoon-like style, Evergood's later works became more fantastical and symbolic. In this painting, a crowd at the Lakehurst Naval Air Station in New Jersey watches a dirigible (zeppelin). It is unclear if the dirigible is starting or ending its journey. Likewise, it is not known whether Evergood created the image before or after the Hindenburg disaster, as both date to 1937.

66

The painting, with its cars, trains, air busses, and hangars, brings to life the Machine Age—with an industrial vibe. The people in the painting convey an air of revelry as if they have just come from an evening at a chop house where martinis and a good meal were on the menu. The air bus, with its grays and dark colors, is reminiscent of Germany's Hindenburg and was my muse for creating a dish centered on a meat with a big bone. Veal is popular in German cooking. I incorporated a cambozola cheese gratin with portobello mushrooms to bring a bit of classical presentation to the dish. The colors of the bleu cheese and dark mushrooms echo the colors in the painting and are a fitting complement to the veal. The red wine mushroom glaze finishes the dish and pays homage to the revelers who topped off their evening with a few cocktails.

—Daniel Medure
Nightfall at the Hangar

The inspiration for my dish was the vibrant colors and delicacy of the Meissen Collection. The piece that specifically inspired me was this stand with chinoiserie scene. In particular, I wanted to feature the fragility of the pieces and all of the rich colors used in the Asian patterns. The dark greens and purples that are seen throughout much of the collection really resonated with me. The green of the palm trees and purple in the clothing immediately brought the ingredients of this dish to mind.

—Andrew Ferenc
Stand

Meissen Porcelain Manufactory
German, 1710
Stand
c. 1760
Porcelain
Gift of Miss Constance I. and Ralph H. Wark
AG.1965.36.117

This Meissen stand features several elaborate scenes. The small scenes around the rim of the stand represent astronomy, zoology, geometry, and chemistry. In the well, the main scene depicts a seated man drinking tea while another plays a dice game. They are joined by a Moorish woman, a monkey, and two standing men in this lush landscape. The entire group is watched over by a fire-breathing flying dragon and two smaller birds. Fanciful scenes like these were assembled into a pattern book called the Schulz Codex. *With 124 sheets and more than 1,000 individual scenes, the* Schulz Codex, *assembled by Meissen artist Johann Gregorius Höroldt (1696 – 1775) around 1723, became the definitive source for Meissen's patterns through 1730.*

Stand

NAPA-WRAPPED CHILI PICKLE & OLIVE SALAD

Andrew Ferenc **ON THE FLY SANDWICHES & STUFF FOOD TRUCK**

Serves 10 - 12

⅔ *cup* sweet chili sauce, preferably Mae Ploy brand
¼ *cup* white vinegar
2 cucumbers, thinly sliced
1 cup Super Colossal Spanish green olives, sliced
½ *cup* pitted kalamata olives, sliced
¼ red onion, thinly sliced
1 large clove garlic, minced
¼ *cup* chopped cilantro, loosely packed
Salt and pepper, to taste
10 to 12 Napa cabbage leaves

In a small mixing bowl, whisk together sweet chili sauce and vinegar. Set aside.

Toss together cucumbers, olives, red onion, garlic, and cilantro. Add vinegar and sweet chili sauce mixture and toss together. Season with salt and pepper, being cautious of salty olives. Refrigerate for 24 hours.

Fill Napa cabbage leaves with salad and serve.

Femme et Mandolin (Woman with a Guitar)

DOROTHY'S FISH BAKE

Daniel Groshell **OCEAN 60**

Serves 4

2 *tablespoons* butter
2 *tablespoons* chopped garlic
2 *tablespoons* chopped shallots
3 Yukon gold potatoes , very thinly sliced
2 *sprigs* oregano, chopped
2 *sprigs* basil, chopped
2 *sprigs* parsley, chopped
2 *sprigs* thyme, chopped
½ *cup* parmesan cheese, grated
1 Bermuda onion, thinly sliced
3 tomatoes, sliced
1 *pound* fresh fish filets or whole fish
2 *cups* white wine
2 *cups* vegetable, chicken, or seafood stock
⅓ *cup* olive oil, or more if desired
2 lemons, sliced into rounds
Kosher salt and freshly ground black pepper, to taste

Preheat oven to 375 degrees.

Coat the bottom of a large porcelain or other oven-proof baking dish with butter. Sprinkle garlic and shallots on the bottom of baking dish.

Arrange potatoes in a single layer on top of garlic and shallots. Season with salt and pepper. Sprinkle herbs on top of potatoes, reserving some for topping the dish. Add parmesan cheese. Arrange onion slices in a single layer and season, then top with tomato slices and season.

Season fish with salt and pepper and place on top of vegetables. Pour white wine and stock around the perimeter of the dish. Drizzle olive oil and place lemon rounds on top of the fish and vegetables. Sprinkle remaining herbs on top of dish.

Cover dish with aluminum foil and bake for 15 to 20 minutes. Exact cooking time will depend on the thickness of the fish and potatoes. Serve family-style in the baking dish, drizzling each serving with pan juices.

Marie Laurencin
French, 1885 – 1956
Femme et Mandolin
(Woman with a Guitar)
1943
Oil on canvas
Gift from Jack and Marcelle Bear
in honor of John S. Bunker
AG.1995.2.1

Marie Laurencin is best known for her images of
women. Through pale colors and distinctive facial
features, Laurencin's women stand out among the
works of her male contemporaries within the Cubist
movement. Her interests in many contemporary
art forms, including music, dance, poetry, and art,
are reflected in her artistic output. A poet, set and
costume designer for the Ballets Russes, and artist,
Laurencin frequently merged her interests through
her work. Here, the woman with her guitar, dressed
in a draped garment with a crown of leaves, can be
interpreted as a modern muse.

66

When viewing this particular piece and learning of the history of the artist's
Parisian, African, and Grecian influence, it became clear that it was a perfect
culinary fit for me. Being a trained classical French chef, I often utilize exotic
inspiration through global flavors to develop my dishes. My culinary motto is
"Technique is Flavor." Therefore, like the painting, which looks very subdued
and simple, there is depth, fluidity, and profound layering not necessarily
visible to the naked eye, but known to the artist in order to create the final
masterpiece. My mother, Dorothy, was an artist and a great influence in my
life. As a family, she often took us on summer trips to Europe, exposing us to
various artistic cultural experiences. It has been a very valuable addition
to my view on culinary arts as another medium of choice. I dedicate this
interpretation to Dorothy.

—Daniel Groshell
Woman with a Guitar

Mosaic with Mask of Silenus

SHRIMP-STUFFED ROASTED TOMATOES WITH PESTO PARMESAN CRUST

Richard Haugk **SUPER FOOD AND BREW**

Serves 6

Olive oil
12 – 16-20 size shrimp, each cut into 4 pieces
1 tablespoon minced garlic
2 handfuls spinach, plus more for serving
1 cup cooked quinoa
4 ounces goat cheese
1 tablespoon pesto, prepared
4 ounces panko
2 ounces parmesan, grated
6 small tomatoes
Balsamic vinegar
Salt and pepper, to taste

Preheat oven to 350 degrees.

Heat olive oil in a skillet and saute shrimp. Add garlic just before shrimp is fully cooked. Remove skillet from heat and add spinach. Stir until the spinach is wilted.

Add quinoa and goat cheese, season with salt and pepper to taste, and thoroughly combine. Place in refrigerator to cool for ten minutes.

In a small bowl, combine pesto, panko, and grated parmesan.

Using a sharp knife, cut off about ⅛ inch from the top of each tomato. Gently scrape out pulp and seeds with a spoon and discard. Put tomatoes, cut sides up, in a baking dish and spoon shrimp mixture into each tomato. Top each tomato with a layer of panko crust and bake until crust is brown and tomatoes are wilted, approximately 20 minutes.

To serve:

Make small bed of spinach greens on a plate. Top with stuffed tomato and drizzle with olive oil and balsamic vinegar.

This ancient Roman mosaic inspired the creation of my dish in many ways.

A mosaic is the combination and marrying of many individual elements

to form a beautiful creation. This is what I envisioned for this stuffed and

roasted tomato dish. The fusion of the delicate coloring and harsh facial

expression on the mask mirror the different ingredients in the dish such

as the mild quinoa and stronger goat cheese. The pairing of the varying

textures and flavors creates a harmonious and cohesive piece.

—Richard Haugk
Mosaic with Mask of Silenus

Roman, Italy
Mosaic with Mask of Silenus
1st century A.D.
Stone, tesserae, and cement
Purchased with funds from the
Morton R. Hirschberg Bequest
AP.1990.19.1

Mosaics, decorative surfaces covered in small pieces of colored stone, marble, or glass, were popular in the ancient world on floors and walls. This small mosaic features a mask of Silenus, a companion to the Greek god of wine, Dionysus. Said to possess great wisdom, Silenus frequently serves as the comedic foil in Greek theatre, where masks were popular props. Silenus is recognizable by his snub nose, round face, and wide eyes.

Tea Bowl and Saucer

DUCK CONFIT – POMEGRANATE SIAO PAO

Blake Burnett **CHEW CHEW FOOD TRUCK**

Serves 4

DUCK CONFIT

4 duck legs and thighs
3 tablespoons coarse salt
1 teaspoon lavender
3 bay leaves, crumbled
6 cloves garlic, smashed and peeled
4 cups duck fat

In a large bowl toss duck with salt, lavender, bay leaves, and garlic until duck is completely coated in spices. Cover and refrigerate for 24 hours.

The next day, preheat oven to 200 degrees.

Remove duck from refrigerator and rub off excess salt mixture. Sear duck, skin side down, in a shallow pan until golden brown.

Heat duck fat in a separate saucepot. Once melted, pour over duck legs and thighs. Cover pan tightly.

Bake for 4 hours. Remove from oven and allow to cool.

Shred duck meat, removing bones and skin.

SIAO PAO FILLING

1 onion, minced
2 tablespoons garlic, minced
2 tablespoons duck fat
4 duck legs and thighs confit, shredded
  (see recipe)
1 tablespoon hoisin sauce
3 tablespoons oyster sauce
2 cups pomegranate juice
2 tablespoons cornstarch slurry

Sauté onions and garlic in duck fat until tender. Add shredded duck confit. Mix in hoisin, oyster sauce, and pomegranate juice. Reduce liquid until it coats the back of a spoon, then add cornstarch slurry to thicken. Reserve excess sauce for garnish.

SIAO PAO

2 cups warm water
1 pouch dry yeast
2 ½ tablespoons sugar
5 cups all-purpose flour
½ cup sugar
1 ¼ tablespoons baking powder
6 tablespoons shortening, room temperature
Thinly sliced scallions, for garnish

Place warm water in a bowl, then add the yeast and 2 ½ tablespoons sugar. Mix well and allow to sit for 10 to 15 minutes (bubbles should form on top).

In a separate bowl mix flour, ½ cup sugar, baking powder, and shortening. Add the yeast-sugar mixture.

Knead the mixture for about 10 minutes or until the texture of the dough becomes smooth. Cover and let the dough rise for at least an hour.

Place the dough in a mixing bowl and knead until very smooth.

Cut dough into individual slices. Using a rolling pin, flatten dough into a thin circle. Place filling in the middle of the circle. Pinch edges of dough together and twist to seal.

Place Siao Pao on wax paper squares and steam for 15 to 20 minutes. Serve with reserved sauce and garnish with scallions.

Johann Gregorius Höroldt
German, 1696 – 1775
Tea Bowl and Saucer
c. 1730
Porcelain
Gift of Miss Constance I. and
Ralph H. Wark
AG.1965.36.126

Augustus the Strong, Elector of Saxony and King of Poland (reg. 1694 – 1733), had a problem. He had spent most of his treasury collecting and importing Asian porcelain, at the time almost as costly as gold. In 1701, he imprisoned scientist Johann Friedrich Böttger (1682 – 1719), who claimed to be able to turn base metals into gold, in an attempt to rectify his financial situation. Although Böttger failed to make gold, he eventually made something just as valuable to Augustus – porcelain. The Meissen Porcelain Manufactory opened in 1710 in the German city of the same name. As the first European firm to successfully manufacture hard-paste porcelain, it closely guarded its secret recipes and formulas.

This tea bowl and saucer was painted by Johann Gregorius Höroldt, who used illustrated travel books to create his fanciful interpretations of life in China, complete with magnificently-dressed men and women as well as exotic plants and animals, like the flying dragon and water buffalo seen on the saucer and bowl, respectively. The saucer also features a likeness of Augustus the Strong being attended to by two Moorish servants.

66

What originally inspired me about the Meissen Collection was seeing people from one culture recreate something from another culture. Everyone who creates, whether it be art, design, or music, will take inspiration from others. Chefs are no exception. I find myself trying to recreate dishes that have caught my eye, or my taste buds if you will, and always find it challenging. Whether it is sourcing products, equipment, or learning techniques, it is never easy. With these challenges come changes and adaptations. This inspired me to use some European techniques and ingredients to recreate one of my favorite Chinese – Filipino dishes: Siao Pao. I only wish that I could have done so with as much class and elegance that the Meissen Factory has done for many centuries.

—Blake Burnett
Tea Bowl and Saucer

66

The subject matter and colors of Agitation *reminded my mother, Araceli,*

of one of the first dishes she made when she arrived in the United States.

She takes a popular Southern ingredient, collard greens, and marries it to

an ingredient she was familiar with from the Philippines—coconut milk.

—*Jaycel Adkins*
Agitation

Agitation

COLLARD GREENS IN COCONUT MILK

Araceli and Jaycel Adkins **CELY'S FILIPINO FOOD**

Serves 2

¼ cup olive oil
1 tablespoon chopped garlic
1 cup chopped onion
1 tablespoon chopped fresh ginger
1 cup chopped fresh tomatoes
3 cups collard greens, woody stems removed, chopped and rinsed
1 – 19 ounce can coconut milk
Bacon, cooked and crumbled *(optional)*
Salt and black pepper, to taste

Heat olive oil in a deep skillet until hot but not smoking. Sauté garlic, onion, ginger, and tomatoes until soft but not browned.

Add collard greens and stir constantly until collards have wilted. Pour coconut milk over greens, add bacon (if desired), reduce heat to low, and cover skillet with a tight-fitting lid.

Simmer greens until coconut milk has thickened, approximately 10 minutes. Season to taste with salt and pepper.

Eugene Savage
American, 1883 – 1978
Agitation
1953
Oil on canvas on Masonite board
with stretcher
Purchased with funds from the
Mae W. Schultz Charitable Lead Trust
AP.2007.2.20

Although American artist Eugene Savage may be best known today for his large public murals, his encounters with Florida's Seminoles dominated nearly 20 years of his career. Savage first visited the Everglades in 1935, at a time when varied interest groups championed conflicting uses for one of Florida's greatest natural resources. The tribe faced threats from every angle, including hunters seeking game, builders wanting cypress and pine, developers building roads and canals for growth, farmers needing fertile soils, and environmentalists lobbying for a national park without the Seminoles. Savage's series of 30 paintings and countless studies focus on this fragile balance. His works cycle from impending destruction to Edenic depictions of the Seminoles living in harmony with the natural world, not as authentic representations of Seminole life but rather as abstracted compositions that evoke mystery and imagination.

Side Chair

AGED DUCK BREAST, HAY SMOKED POTATOES, PICKLED
GREEN STRAWBERRIES AND PURSLANE, ROSE WATER AIR

Waylon Rivers **BLACK SHEEP RESTAURANT**

Serves 2

AGED DUCK BREAST

1 whole duck
Kosher Salt

To age the duck, hang in the refrigerator with a long piece of butcher's twine wrapped around the breast, tying a knot beneath the wings. Let it hang in the fridge for 7 days with a sheet tray underneath lined with a layer of salt to catch any liquid that comes from the duck. The salt will help absorb any unpleasant odor from the liquid.

Remove the duck from the fridge and butcher the duck to give you two whole duck breasts and 2 leg quarters. Save the leg quarters in the freezer for later use, such as duck confit.

HAY SMOKED POTATOES

6 to 8 fingerling potatoes, cut on a bias into
   bite size pieces
Kosher salt
4 black peppercorns
4 sprigs thyme
1 bay leaf
½ sprig fresh rosemary
Fresh hay, purchased from a feed store

Place the potatoes in a small saucepot and add cold water to just cover potatoes. Season the water with a fair amount of salt. Wrap the remaining ingredients in a piece of cheesecloth or coffee filter and tie with butcher's twine. Place in the pot with the potatoes. Bring the water to a light boil and check the salt level of the water once the salt has dissolved. It should taste slightly less salty than pasta boiling water.

Once the potatoes reach a boil, immediately reduce to a simmer and cook until the potatoes are fork tender but not falling apart. Once they are cooked, strain off the water, discard the cheesecloth, and set potatoes aside.

To finish the potatoes, line a large stock pot with fresh hay. Wrap the potatoes in cheesecloth and heat the pot to get the hay to start smoking. Once the smoke starts, wrap foil around the lid to trap the smoke and let the potatoes smoke for 30 minutes or until a desired smoke flavor is achieved.

PICKLED GREEN STRAWBERRIES

1 pint green (unripe) strawberries
¼ cup champagne vinegar
¼ cup white sugar
¼ cup water
¼ teaspoon kosher salt

Remove the leaves from the strawberries. Place vinegar, sugar, water, and salt in a pot and heat the pickling brine until the sugar and salt have dissolved completely. Pour over the strawberries. Place in the refrigerator in a small container for 12 to 24 hours before using. They will last up to 2 weeks submerged in the liquid in your fridge.

ROSE WATER AIR

200 grams rose water
8 grams white sugar
2 grams kosher salt
2 grams soy lecithin
½ gram xanthan gum

Combine all ingredients and blend until they dissolve. Whip with a stick blender on high speed until sufficient foam is formed. Allow to drain for 2 minutes and for foam to stabilize.

To finish the dish:

Aged Duck Breast
Pickled Green Strawberries
1 cup purslane leaves
½ tablespoon extra virgin olive oil
Hay Smoked Potatoes
Rose Water Air
Kosher salt and pepper

Season the duck breasts with kosher salt and pepper, and place in a cold cast iron pan skin side down. Slowly bring up the heat of the pan to render the fat out of the skin until a crispy texture has been achieved.

While the skin is rendering, baste the flesh of the duck with the fat that is rendering to cook to desired temperature. If a medium-well or well-done temperature is desired, then finish in a 400 degree oven for 6 to 8 minutes after the skin has become crispy. Allow the duck to rest on a plate while you prepare the rest.

Halve 5 to 6 strawberries and place in a mixing bowl with purslane leaves. Pour 2 tablespoons of the pickling liquid into the bowl along with olive oil and season to taste with salt.

Slice the duck and lay one whole duck breast on each plate. Surround the duck with 5 to 6 pieces of potatoes, and ½ of the strawberry and purslane salad. Then add a few spoonfuls of rose water air to the plate.

George Walton
Scottish, 1867 – 1933
Side Chair
c. 1900
Satinwood with inlay and
contemporary upholstery
Made for Liberty & Co., London
Gift of James and Diane Burke
in memory of Thomas H. Jacobsen
AG.2003.7.1

*George Walton was one of the leading
architects and designers of the Arts and
Crafts movement. He established his own
firm, George Walton & Co., Ecclesiastical
and House Decorators, in Glasgow in 1888.
Walton's broad reach extended from
comprehensive interior design projects
to individual elements like wallpaper, glass,
carpets, and furniture, including this side
chair made for London-based retailer
Liberty & Co.*

"

When looking at the chair, which was crafted by a Scottish man, I made an immediate connection. The scene on the chair immediately jumped out to me as spring on a plate. The game bird with the flowers and fruit not only made a fine looking print for a chair but a great combination on a plate. I wanted the dish to represent the vision of nature on the chair as well as to invoke your senses with the smell of the smoked hay and the scent of the rose water.

—Waylon Rivers
Side Chair

66

Light Wash *immediately spoke to me. The calm serenity this piece*

induces is comforting, while still showcasing a tediousness necessary for the

"simple life." The dish I created is a perfect balance of simplicity with a twist

of creativity. The watercolor, like my dish, takes me to a place of bliss which

I hope, and can only assume, Wyeth intended for us as well.

—Arielle Coutu
Light Wash

Light Wash

A DAY IN THE LIFE

Arielle Coutu **TAPA THAT**

Serves 1

Gorgonzola cheese
⅛ *cup* parmesan cheese, shredded
1 square of wheatgrass
Handful arugula, or other fresh spring greens
2 fresh mission figs, quartered
4 – 5 white asparagus tips, blanched
1 – 2 slices prosciutto, thinly sliced
A drizzle of white balsamic glaze
Walnuts, toasted and crumbled
Cracked black peppercorns

Place gorgonzola in freezer while preparing the parmesan "basket."

Heat a non-stick pan over medium-low heat. Spread the Parmesan in the center of the pan in a single, slightly laced layer to create a basket effect. Once the edges start to bubble and the cheese begins to melt together, use a non-stick spatula to flip the cheese. Allow to cook for another minute or so.

While cheese is still hot, drape it over the bottom of a well-oiled glass and form it to create a basket. Remove parmesan basket from the glass once the cheese is cool and holds its basket shape.

To assemble dish, place square of wheatgrass in one corner of a large platter. Carefully set the parmesan basket on top of the wheatgrass. Fill basket with arugula and place a couple figs in and around the salad. Nestle some figs in the wheatgrass.

Stack the asparagus tips like firewood in the opposite corner of the plate and place rolled up shreds of prosciutto around the tips. Drizzle balsamic glaze from corner to corner and sprinkle the walnuts over the plate.

Remove gorgonzola from freezer and shave thin sheets of the cheese over the salad. Crack black peppercorns over dish.

Andrew Wyeth
American, 1917 – 2009
Light Wash
1961
Watercolor on paper
Gift of Ms. Gillian Attfield
AG.1980.6.1

Andrew Wyeth was part of an American dynasty of artists. His father, N.C. Wyeth, was a noted illustrator. His son, Jamie, and sisters, Carolyn and Henriette, all received recognition for their talents as well. Light Wash captures the solitude of an afternoon in Chadds Ford, Pennsylvania, the Wyeths' home town. As laundry dries in the dappled sunlight and is animated by a breeze, a dog naps in the grass next to a straw basket.

© Andrew Wyeth

Takashi Soga
Japanese, b. 1952
Sea of the Ear Rings
2008
Metal
Gift of Dudley D. Johnson in memory
of Dudley D. Johnson, Jr. (1961 – 2004)
AG.2008.3.1

Takashi Soga, born in Japan, is recognized globally for his kinetic sculptures that use gravity to challenge spatial relationships. He explains, "The title Sea of the Ear *is the metaphor of my main concept – gravity. We have the sensor to feel gravity in the ear. I focus on the gravity to make unordinary space...The upper ring is moving up and down slowly by the wind, but this movement is something unusual...[the ring] seems to be independent in the air. When people first notice the movement, the space is changed dynamically, which is a new experience...The upper ring is released from the hold of gravity and breaks our fixed idea about how space changes. It makes us feel free."[1]*

"

My goal is always to delight those for whom I cook. Guests at my restaurant, Blue Bamboo, are often happy to see my menu change regularly, and get better with each visit. My work often features Asian flavors based on classic American cooking techniques. Some reviews have labeled my work as "ostensibly Chinese," but I am also known to make a killer Italian Malfatti or outstanding Cuban Mojo. I always study both the cultural technique and historic flavor of a dish before creating my own recipe.

In this dish, I am inspired by the iconic Sea of the Ear Rings *by Takashi Soga. The kinetic structure reminds me of the rings of a jalapeno pepper, which offer a visual preview of this dish's flavorful heat. This work stands outdoors at the front of the Cummer Museum, previewing the beautiful art inside the Museum. When tasting this dish, you will enjoy savory, sweet, spicy, and sour flavors.*

—Dennis Chan
Sea of the Ear Rings

Sea of the Ear Rings

SEA OF THE EAR RINGS FISH

Dennis Chan **BLUE BAMBOO**

Serves 2

1 whole fish, about 1 pound, cleaned and scaled,
    or an 8-ounce filet
Neutral oil, for frying
2 shallots, chopped
2 *tablespoons* chopped fresh ginger
2 *cloves* garlic, chopped
1 *tablespoon* tamarind paste
2 *tablespoons* fish sauce
3 *tablespoons* sugar
¼ *cup* water
2 – 4 red jalapeño peppers, seeded and
    sliced into rings
3 *sprigs* cilantro
Salt and pepper, to taste
Cilantro leaves, for garnish
Steamed rice, for serving

Score the fish at an angle through skin and flesh on both sides to allow meat to cook evenly. Season with salt and pepper.

Add enough oil to a large pan to cover half of the fish when submerged. Fry the fish at 350 degrees for approximately 10 minutes on the first side. Flip the fish over and fry remaining side until done, approximately 5 minutes. Remove fish from pan and place on paper towels to drain.

Heat a wok or large pan over medium heat. Add a teaspoon of oil and saute shallots, ginger, and garlic. Stir to release aromatics. Add tamarind paste, fish sauce, sugar, and water. Mix well and bring to a boil. Add jalapenos and cook, tossing, just until wilted. Taste and adjust seasonings. The sauce should have a balance of sweet, spicy, and sour flavors.

Pour the sauce over the fish and garnish with cilantro leaves. Serve with steamed rice.

The Cummer Oak

HERB GRILLED QUAIL, COUNTRY SAUSAGE-CORNBREAD STUFFING, GOAT CHEESE, MOREL MUSHROOM GRAVY, SPICED WALNUTS, FIDDLEHEAD FERNS, AND ROASTED BABY BEETS

Jamey Evoniuk and Chris Irvin **CUMMER CAFÉ and THE CHEF'S GARDEN CATERING & EVENTS**

Serves 4

HERB GRILLED QUAIL WITH COUNTRY SAUSAGE-CORNBREAD STUFFING

Extra virgin olive oil
1 pound country sausage, casing removed and crumbled
2 ribs celery, chopped
1 red bell pepper, chopped
1 large Vidalia onion, chopped
3 cloves garlic, chopped
1 tablespoon Creole spice
2 cups rosemary cornbread, cubed and oven dried
1 cup chicken stock
2 eggs
4 ounces goat cheese
1 tablespoon chopped thyme
1 tablespoon chopped rosemary
4 semi-boneless quail
Extra virgin olive oil
1 tablespoon chopped thyme
1 tablespoon chopped rosemary
1 tablespoon chopped sage
Salt and pepper, to taste

Heat oil in a large pan over medium-high heat. Add sausage, celery, bell pepper, and onion, then cook until onion is translucent. Add garlic, Creole spice, cornbread, and chicken stock. Fold in eggs, goat cheese, and fresh herbs. Season with salt and pepper.

Meanwhile, marinate the quail in olive oil, thyme, rosemary, and sage. Cover and refrigerate for 1 hour. Remove from marinade and season with salt and pepper.

Preheat oven to 400 degrees.

Stuff each quail with cornbread stuffing. Using a thin piece of foil, wrap the midsection of the quail to keep stuffing in and the folded legs in. Place on the grill, breast side down, for two minutes, then flip and cook on the other side for two minutes. Finish quail in the oven for 7 minutes, or until it reaches an internal temperature of 165 degrees.

MUSHROOM GRAVY

2 tablespoons butter
3 cloves garlic, minced
2 shallots, minced
¼ pound fresh morel mushrooms, if available *(or dried mushrooms reconstituted in hot stock)*
½ cup brandy
½ cup chicken stock
½ cup heavy cream
1 teaspoon chopped fresh thyme
Salt and pepper, to taste

Sauté garlic and shallots in butter until fragrant. Add morels and cook for 1 minute. Add brandy and reduce until almost dry, add chicken stock and reduce by half, then add heavy cream and thyme and reduce by a quarter. Remove some of the morels from the sauce and puree the rest of the sauce in a blender until smooth. Taste and adjust seasoning.

SPICED WALNUTS

1 egg white
¾ cup sugar
Cinnamon, to taste
Cayenne, to taste
1 pound walnuts

Preheat oven to 325 degrees. Lightly grease a half sheet pan.

Whisk egg white until frothy. In a separate bowl, mix sugar, cinnamon, and cayenne. Coat walnuts thoroughly in egg white then toss in sugar mixture. Pour walnuts onto greased sheet pan and bake for 10 minutes. Stir walnuts, then return to oven and cook another 5 minutes. Repeat one more time, stirring walnuts and cooking for an additional 5 minutes (walnuts should bake for a total of 20 minutes). Remove from oven and let cool.

To serve:

8 baby beets, roasted and peeled
8 fiddlehead ferns, blanched and sautéed with butter and shallots
Sliced radishes
Salt and pepper, to taste

Serve quail with mushroom gravy, roasted baby beets, and fiddlehead ferns. Garnish with spiced walnuts and radishes.

The Cummer Oak exemplifies beauty, strength, and wisdom. It pays tribute to the past while reaching and connecting to the future. This is an heirloom dish that takes classic cuisine and adds character and intensity to it. The roots of the tree are quite directly represented with beets, a classic root vegetable, but more metaphorically through the cornbread stuffing which is a generational dish shared from my grandmother to me. Likewise, the quail represents ethereal beauty very directly, while also more figuratively representing growth and reaching towards the future.

—Jamey Evoniuk and Chris Irvin
The Cummer Oak

The Cummer Oak

With its spread of approximately 150 feet, the Cummer Oak (Live oak/Quercus virginiana) is estimated to be between 175 and 200 years old. Like many live oaks of the Gulf South, the Cummer Oak's limbs are draped with Spanish moss (Tillandsia usneoides) and resurrection fern (Pleopeltis polypodioides), named for its changed appearance from brown to green after a rainstorm.

The Italian Garden

HANDMADE GNOCCHI WITH SWEET PEA PURÉE, OYSTER MUSHROOMS, AND CRISPY GUANCIALE

Tom Gray **MOXIE KITCHEN + COCKTAILS**

Serves 4

HANDMADE GNOCCHI

2 large Idaho potatoes (about 1 pound), peeled and cut into 2-inch pieces
2 cups all-purpose flour, plus more as needed for proper consistency
½ cup finely grated Parmesan
2 pinches white pepper
1 teaspoon sea salt
¼ teaspoon freshly grated nutmeg
1 large farm egg, whisked

Place potatoes in a large pot with enough water to cover by one inch. Bring to a boil, reduce to a simmer, and cook until fork tender. Rice potatoes through a food mill, distributing them evenly onto a large cutting board.

Allow riced potatoes to cool until lukewarm. This allows the excess moisture to evaporate.

Sift flour over potatoes in an even layer, which should be about the same height as the potatoes. Sprinkle Parmesan, white pepper, sea salt, and nutmeg on top of potatoes and flour. Fold dry ingredients together on top of cutting board using an offset spatula until well incorporated. Form mixture into a pile and create a well in the center. Pour whisked egg into the well and slowly incorporate into dry ingredients by hand until dough is crumbly and begins to come together. If dough is sticky and hard to work with, add more flour as needed. Form dough into a loaf and let rest for 30 minutes. Cut off small pieces of dough from the loaf and roll into ½-inch thick ropes. With a sharp knife, cut each rope into ½-inch pieces. Lightly pinch the center of each piece to create a small indention. Dust lightly with flour.*

Bring a large pot of water to a low boil. Cook gnocchi in boiling water until they begin to float.

Continue to cook for 1 to 2 minutes more.

Strain and set aside until ready to use.

*At this point you can freeze gnocchi in a single layer on a sheet tray. Once frozen, gnocchi can be stored in an air-tight ziploc or vacuum-sealed bag in the freezer for up to 6 months. Cook frozen gnocchi following steps above.

SWEET PEA PURÉE

10 ounces fresh or frozen sweet peas
¾ cup heavy cream, warmed and divided
1 teaspoon kosher salt
⅛ teaspoon white pepper

Blanch peas in salted boiling water for about 1 to 2 minutes. Shock peas in an ice bath to stop the cooking process and preserve the bright green color. Strain peas, and place in a blender. Add ½ cup hot heavy cream and purée until smooth. Stir in salt and white pepper and set aside. When ready to serve, slowly reheat the purée and the remaining ¼ cup heavy cream over medium heat, stirring constantly, until well incorporated and hot.

CRISPY GUANCIALE

4 ounces guanciale, pancetta, or bacon, very thinly sliced

Ask your local butcher or deli counter to slice the meat for you in order to get it paper thin.

Preheat oven to 250 degrees.

Arrange slices in a single layer on a parchment-lined sheet tray. Bake until crispy, 20 to 25 minutes, without allowing them to brown too much.

To finish and plate:

3 tablespoons canola oil, divided
8 ounces oyster mushrooms, cleaned and broken into individual pieces
4 cups Gnocchi, blanched
1 cup vegetable broth
½ cup grated Pecorino cheese, plus more for garnishing
2 tablespoons butter, softened
1 cup warm Sweet Pea Purée
Crispy Guanciale
8 snow peas, blanched and julienned on the bias
¼ cup assorted sweet herbs *(basil, tarragon, dill)*, pea shoots, or
   microgreens, for garnishing
Kosher salt and freshly ground black pepper

Heat 1 tablsepoon canola oil in a large nonstick skillet over medium-high heat. Add mushrooms and sauté until slightly brown and tender. Season to taste with salt and set aside on a plate lined with a paper towel. Wipe the pan clean if necessary.

Heat remaining 2 tablespoons canola oil over medium-high heat. When oil is hot, add gnocchi to the skillet and allow it to sear, without stirring, until golden brown. Flip gnocchi and sear on the other side.

Add sautéed mushrooms and cook until warmed through. Add vegetable broth to the pan, cooking a few minutes more until heated through and gnocchi is plumped. Remove gnocchi from heat and swirl in the Pecorino and butter until both are melted and incorporated. Season with salt and pepper, to taste.

To serve, place ¼ cup of the warm Sweet Pea Purée in the bottom of a shallow bowl. Using a slotted spoon, place about 1 cup of the gnocchi and mushroom mixture on top of the purée. Top each bowl with Crispy Guanciale, julienned snow peas, and grated Pecorino. Garnish with sweet herbs, pea shoots, or microgreens and serve.

The Italian Garden

Arthur and Ninah Cummer built the Italian Garden in 1931. The couple had recently returned from Italy, where Mrs. Cummer became enchanted by the Villa Gamberaia, just outside of Florence.

Designed by noted landscape architect Ellen Biddle Shipman (1869 – 1950), the Italian Garden echoes the design of Villa Gamberaia's gardens, with its long pools, clipped hedges, and vine-covered gloriette. Although Shipman's involvement in the Italian Garden initially faded from history, her role became apparent when a set of plans was discovered in the designer's archives at Cornell University. This led to a restoration of the Garden in the 1990s.

The Italian Garden is named in memory of Margaret Baker Berg.

66

There is a parallel between my appreciation of the Italian Garden's beauty, its layout, symmetry, curves, arches, and lines, and a similarity to how I work with ingredients. I choose ingredients for a dish based on flavor first, and also for their color, texture, shape, and visual interest when plated together.

The Garden is a creative, living expression of a framework that has grown with time and the seasons. While the Garden was designed and planted many years ago, today one can enjoy its evolving beauty, much as a person can enjoy a classic dish with slightly new ways of interpreting the ingredients or techniques used to prepare it.

I spent many hours with my son when he was young in this Garden. Together, we explored the variety of colors, shapes, textures, and smells, and I marveled at his delight in the discoveries he found. This is similar to how we as humans enjoy food and flavors. Ingredients bring out different nuances and the layers of aroma, texture, visual appeal, and taste can excite every sense.

—Tom Gray
The Italian Garden

Anna Hyatt Huntington
American, 1876 – 1973
Diana of the Hunt
1922; recast 1960
Bronze
Gift of Anna Hyatt Huntington
AG.1961.15.1
*Support for the restoration of this sculpture
has been provided by the Henry Luce Foundation,
FOCUS Cummer, Mrs. Barbara H. Arnold,
Mrs. Walter A. McRae, Jr., and
Mr. and Mrs. Robert T. Shircliff.*

*Given to the Cummer Museum in celebration of
its opening in 1961,* Diana of the Hunt *has come to
be an important element of the Museum's historic
Gardens. Artist Anna Hyatt Huntington, who gifted
the sculpture to the Museum, was highly regarded
for her skill in depicting human and animal
anatomy.* Diana of the Hunt *combines these two
strengths. Perched atop a globe, Diana, Roman
goddess of women and patroness of the hunt,
shoots an arrow towards the moon as her hunting
dog jumps in excitement.*

❝

When I first saw this sculpture I decided to do a skewer to represent the arrow. Diana is the Roman goddess of the hunt, so I knew I could draw plenty of ideas from her lore. I chose Cornish hen because it would be small enough to be recognized as the game bird even after being skewered. The Romans' primary diet consisted of large amounts of bread so a bread pudding became a solid foundation for the dish. Diana herself was associated with oak, so I decided to make a Chardonnay reduction which was aged in oak barrels. The remaining elements of the dish come from a list I found of common foods in Ancient Rome. They are combined it a way that expressed my culinary style while being within the ability of a home cook.

—Joseph Hegland
Diana of the Hunt

Diana of the Hunt

HEN OF AVENTINE HILL

Joseph Hegland **JJ'S BISTRO**

4 cups cubed whole grain bread
8 tablespoons butter, divided
3 leeks, thoroughly rinsed and chopped
6 cloves garlic, chopped
1 quart chicken stock, divided
1 bunch flat leaf parsley, chopped
2 eggs
Cooking oil
2 Cornish game hens, quartered
12 ounces heirloom carrots
2 cups chardonnay
12 ounces fresh or frozen English peas
Salt and pepper, to taste

In a 250 degree oven, bake the bread for 1 hour to dry it out.

Increase oven temperature to 325 degrees.

Heat 2 tablespoons butter, leeks, garlic, and a pinch of salt in a small saucepot. Cook slowly over low heat until leeks have softened.

In a large mixing bowl, combine 2 cups chicken stock, the dried bread, leeks, garlic, parsley, and eggs, then knead until all liquid is absorbed into the bread. Grease a large muffin tin lightly with oil. Fill four of the muffin slots with the bread mixture. Cover with aluminum foil and bake for 1 hour.

Pat the Cornish hens dry with a paper towel and season liberally with salt and pepper. Refrigerate until needed.

Bring a large pot of salted water to a boil and blanch the carrots until they bend slightly under pressure. Drain and refrigerate until needed.

Approximately 45 minutes before you wish to eat, remove the bread pudding from the muffin tin. Place on a baking sheet and warm in a 350 degree oven.

In a large sauté pan set over medium-high heat, add 4 tablespoons of butter and 2 tablespoons of oil and allow the butter to melt. Cook the hen in batches of four pieces at a time, starting skin side down. Once golden brown, flip the hens and cook for one minute on the other side. Places hen pieces on a baking sheet and place in the oven.

Drain off the excess fat from the saute pan. Add one cup of stock and wine to the pan, then allow to reduce by ⅔ over medium heat. Add 4 tablespoons butter and swirl until butter melts into the sauce.

In a separate sauté pan, bring the remaining cup of stock and 2 tablespoons butter to a full boil. Add the peas and carrots with a pinch of salt and cook, stirring frequently, until the liquid has fully evaporated and the vegetables have begun to brown slightly.

To serve, place the bread pudding in the center of a plate and surround with the vegetables. Place a leg quarter directly on top of the bread pudding followed by a breast; use a skewer to hold them in place. Generously spoon the sauce over the hen and vegetables, then garnish with the remaining parsley.

Ponce de León in Florida

PAN SEARED FLOUNDER WITH CITRUS DATIL POACHED SHRIMP

Jeffrey Stanford **THE BLIND RABBIT, A BURGER AND WHISKEY BAR**

Serves 2

PAN SEARED FLOUNDER

2 – 6 ounce flounder filets
2 teaspoons Creole spice
2 teaspoons sea salt
½ teaspoon black pepper
2 tablespoons whole butter
White wine
Lemon

Season both sides of the flounder filets with Creole spice, salt, and pepper.

Heat butter in a medium saute pan on medium-high heat. Gently place the seasoned fish in the pan and cook for two minutes per side. Finish with a drizzle of white wine and a squeeze of fresh lemon.

CITRUS DATIL POACHED SHRIMP

1 cup white wine
Juice of ½ lime
Juice of ½ lemon
Juice of ½ orange
1 datil chili pepper, split
2 whole fresh local shrimp, head on
Creole spice
Sea salt

Place wine, citrus juices, and datil pepper in a small saucepot and bring to a simmer. Cook for 5 minutes to allow the flavors to infuse the liquid. Reduce liquid to a simmer (it should read 180 to 200 degrees on thermometer). Poach shrimp in small batches for 3 minutes

and season with a little creole spice and sea salt once they are removed from the liquid. Serve immediately.

CITRUS BEURRE BLANC

2 cups white wine
1 shallot, brunoise
Juice of ½ lime
Juice of ½ lemon
Juice of ½ orange
1 sprig fresh thyme
¼ cup heavy whipping cream
½ pound whole butter, cold
Salt and pepper, to taste

Place wine, shallot, citrus juices, and thyme sprig in a small saucepot. Reduce the liquid by half over medium-low heat. Once the liquid has reduced, add the heavy whipping cream and reduce again by half. Remove the sauce from the heat and add the whole butter while whisking until the butter is incorporated. Season with salt and pepper.

SWEET YELLOW CORN PUREE

½ cup heavy whipping cream
4 cups fresh roasted yellow corn
2 tablespoons whole butter
Salt and pepper, to taste

Place cream in a small saucepot and warm over medium-low heat. Add corn and cook until the corn and cream are hot. Season with

salt and pepper, to taste and add the butter. Puree mixture in a blender until smooth.

SUMMER SUCCOTASH

1 tablespoon extra virgin olive oil
1 tablespoon chopped garlic
6 fingerling potatoes, boiled and sliced
1 cup white acre peas
½ cup sweet yellow corn
6 okra, sliced
6 haricot verts, cut on the bias
6 baby heirloom tomatoes, quartered
2 tablespoons chopped fresh cilantro
2 tablespoons sliced green onions
1 tablespoon whole butter
Salt and pepper, to taste

Heat olive oil in a saute pan over medium-high heat and saute garlic until light brown. Add the potatoes, white acre peas, corn, okra, and haricot verts. Cook for 3 to 4 minutes then add tomatoes, cilantro, green onions, salt, and pepper, to taste. Finish by stirring in the butter until it melts.

To serve, place sweet yellow corn puree in the bottom of a shallow bowl. Spoon succotash over corn and top with flounder, then poached shrimp. Finish with a generous drizzle of citrus beurre blanc.

Thomas Moran
American, 1837 – 1926
Ponce de León in Florida
1877 – 1878
Oil on canvas
Acquired for the people of Florida by the
Frederick H. Schultz family and Barnett Banks, Inc.
with additional funds from the Cummer Council
AP.1996.2.1

Thomas Moran aspired to become one of America's first history painters. Known for creating large-scale canvases infused with noble stories, history painters were traditionally respected in European artistic circles as the more important of their peers. Moran wanted to paint scenes that depicted momentous events in America's relatively short past, and hoped this painting of the Spanish conquistador Juan Ponce de León (c. 1474 – 1521) in the company of native Floridians would hang in the House of Representatives in Washington, D.C. Instead, magnate Henry Flagler (1830 – 1913) purchased the work for one of his new hotels in St. Augustine, the Ponce de León. Despite the fact that Moran depicted Plains Indians rather than the Timucua who would have inhabited Florida at the time, he represented Florida's lush landscape accurately.

66

This painting is a mythic depiction of the coming together of the Spanish and the Timucua Indian cultures. I saw beauty in the blending of cultures and my dish provides a blending of the flavors from both of these worlds.

—Jeffrey Stanford

Ponce de León in Florida

66

I chose this woodblock print of Hodemi-no-Mikoto, *a popular story in both Japan and my native China that has been retold in books, on television, and in video games. The image brought back wonderful childhood memories of an ancient story that has become a part of Asian culture. I was able to recreate the image of the giant fish using Japanese snapper. I filleted half the fish and laid the meat in waves beneath the body to resemble the strong seas depicted in the print. I sculpted cucumbers, and placed mint and lemons to replicate the most vivid colors in the print.*

—Jason Chen
Biyu Suikoden
(Beauty and Valor in
the Novel Suikoden):
Hodemi-no-Mikoto

Biyu Suikoden (Beauty and Valor in the Novel Suikoden): Hodemi-no-Mikoto

RED SNAPPER, CUCUMBER, LEMON, GINGER, WASABI, AND PONZU/YUZU SAUCE

Jason Chen **KAZU**

Tsukioka Yoshitoshi
Japanese, 1839 – 1892
**Biyu Suikoden
(Beauty and Valor in
the Novel Suikoden):
Hodemi-no-Mikoto**
1867
Woodblock print on paper
The Dennis C. Hayes Collection
AG.1998.4.52

During the 19th century, Japanese playwrights and artists looked to history for inspiration. A popular retelling of the Chinese novel Suikoden ("The Water Margin"), *translated into Japanese at the end of the 18th century, launched a craze that spread to theatre and books, as well as merchandise like kites. The story tells of the adventures of a legendary group of 108 Chinese outlaws during the 12th century. The group, much like the legendary Western character Robin Hood, supports the common people through their crimes.*

Here, artist Tsukioka Yoshitoshi represents Hodemi-no-Mikoto, who lost his brother's fishing hook. In his descent to the bottom of the sea to find the hook, he met Toyo-Tame, daughter of the sea god, whom he later married.

Sushi-grade whole red snapper
Assorted sushi grade fish
1 jalapeno pepper, seeded and sliced into
  thin rounds
1 lemon, sliced into thin rounds
Thinly sliced radish
Pickled ginger
Wasabi
Ponzu/yuzu sauce

Artfully arrange fish on a large platter with jalapeno, lemon, and radish. Serve with pickled ginger, wasabi, and ponzu/yuzu sauce.

"

Initially my inspiration came from the geometrical square shape of the painting as well as the layering of bold colors and brush strokes. After reading the artist's statement I was intrigued with his travels and started thinking of my own culinary experiences through Europe. One specific memory is of when my wife and I were traveling through the South of France and we stopped for lunch. Sitting out overlooking the Mediterranean we enjoyed a local Salade Niçoise. Although simple, this dish was complex with its layering of ingredients and flavors. We enjoyed this local dish so much I decided to recreate this experience as the artist did with his own personal encounters.

—Rick Laughlin
Home

Home

TUNA CARPACCIO, BLACK OLIVE TAPIOCA, BRUSSELS SPROUTS, GREEN BEANS,
PURPLE POTATOES, SHERRY VINAIGRETTE, QUAIL EGGS

Rick Laughlin **SALT RESTAURANT**

Serves 4

TUNA CARPACCIO

10 ounce tuna loin
4 tablespoons olive oil
Salt and pepper

Cut the tuna loin into 1-inch wide x 3-inch long portions. Season with salt and pepper.

Heat a medium sauté pan. Add olive oil and bring to the smoke point.

Sear tuna for 2 to 3 seconds on all four sides. Remove to a plate lined with paper towels to drain the fat. Place tuna in refrigerator to cool for 15 minutes.

After tuna is cooled, slice into quarter inch pieces and reserve.

Spread out 12 inches of plastic wrap. Place 6 pieces of cut tuna into the center of the wrap. Cover the tuna with 12 inches of plastic wrap.

Pound out tuna with a meat pallet, pounding from the inside moving outward. Once tuna is pounded out use a rolling pin to smooth to ⅛" thick. Cut to desired portion size.

BLACK OLIVE TAPIOCA

2 cups Kalamata olives, pitted and rinsed
1 cup tapioca
4 ounces hot water
2 cups vegetable oil
Preheat oven to 200 degrees.

Spread out Kalamata olives on a sheet pan and dehydrate in oven for 4 hours. Cool to room temperature.

Using a food processor, pulse olives until they resemble ground coffee. Reserve.

Bring 1 gallon of water to a boil. Add tapioca and boil for 8 minutes. Pass tapioca through a strainer and rinse under cold water until the water runs clear.

Place half the cooked tapioca in a blender and reserve the remaining in a medium mixing bowl. Add ground olives and 4 ounces of hot water to blender, then puree until smooth. Add mixture to the mixing bowl with the remaining half of tapioca. Mix well and spread mixture evenly out on a silpat.

Place in oven and dehydrate at 200 degrees for 4 hours. Break into pieces.

Heat the vegetable oil until it starts to smoke. Add the tapioca to oil and fry until it puffs. Drain on a paper towel and store in an airtight container.

BRUSSELS SPROUTS

1 cup vegetable oil
10 Brussels sprouts
Fine sea salt

In a saucepot, heat oil to 325 degrees. Peel outer leaves of the sprouts, reserving the hearts. Fry leaves until crispy and drain on paper towels. Season with fine sea salt.

GREEN BEANS

20 green beans
Kosher salt, to taste

Bring 1 gallon water to a boil. Add enough salt to the water so it tastes salty like the ocean. Add the green beans and cook until tender. Shock the beans in ice water, then strain and reserve.

PURPLE POTATOES

4 purple potatoes
Kosher salt, to taste

Peel the potatoes. Using a melon baller, scoop out small balls from the potatoes, reserving in water until ready to cook.

Bring 1 gallon water to a boil. Add enough salt to the water so it tastes salty like the ocean. Add the potato balls and cook until tender. Shock the potatoes in ice water, then strain and reserve.

SHERRY VINAIGRETTE

½ cup caramelized sweet onions
2 tablespoons sherry vinegar
2 teaspoons Dijon mustard
½ teaspoon kosher salt
⅛ teaspoon ground white pepper
2 teaspoons honey
6 ounces blend oil (25% extra virgin, 75% canola)

Add onions to a blender and puree until smooth. Add vinegar, mustard, salt, pepper, and honey, then puree. While motor is running, slowly add the oil until vinaigrette is emulsified.

QUAIL EGGS

6 quail eggs
2 cups water
½ cup white vinegar

Place all ingredients in a small saucepan and bring to a boil. Simmer for 3 minutes. Remove eggs to an ice bath. Peels eggs once they are completely cool.

To serve:

Place tuna on a flat plate. Toss Brussels sprouts leaves, green beans, and purple potatoes in sherry vinaigrette. Arrange vegetables, tapioca, and halved quail eggs on top of tuna and serve.

Howard Hodgkin
British, b. 1932
Home
2001
Hand-painted liftground etching
with aquatint and carborundum
Gift of Russell B. Newton, Jr. and
Joannie Newton
AG.2012.3.1

British artist Howard Hodgkin aspired to become an artist at a young age, especially after visiting the Museum of Modern Art in New York and seeing work by Henri Matisse (1869 – 1954), Pablo Picasso (1881 – 1973), and Stuart Davis (1892 – 1964). Much of his work references experiences in his own life. Hodgkin describes his work as "representational pictures of emotional experiences." [2]

The Bronco Buster

FLORIDA CRACKER CAKE

Adam Burnett **KNEAD BAKESHOP**

SPICY PEPPER JAM

For the pepper juice:

35 mixed hot peppers like datil, jalapeno, or red chile,
 seeded and chopped
392 grams white vinegar
280 grams water

Combine all ingredients in a saucepan and bring to a boil. Cover, reduce to a simmer, and let simmer for 15 minutes. Remove from heat and allow to rest, covered, for 30 minutes.

For the jelly:

All the pepper juice, peppers included
1,000 grams granulated sugar
1 – 3 ounce pouch liquid pectin

In an 8 quart pot, bring juice to just below a simmer. Add the sugar and stir constantly until it reaches a boil. Add the pectin and continue stirring, at a boil, for 1 minute.

Transfer jam to a heat resistant container and allow to cool. Stir jam every five minutes so the peppers are evenly distributed. Cover and cool in fridge overnight. The jam should be made at least a day ahead of time.

CORNBREAD CAKE

450 grams butter, at room temperature
530 grams granulated sugar
7 grams sea salt
10 large eggs
10 grams vanilla
250 grams all-purpose flour
330 grams fine yellow cornmeal
Bourbon, for brushing finished cake

Preheat oven to 350 degrees.

Butter and flour two 9-inch cake pans.

In a stand mixer using paddle attachment, cream together butter, sugar, and salt on medium speed until light and fluffy, about 5 minutes.

On low speed, add eggs one at a time, scraping bottom of bowl between each addition. Add vanilla.

Mix together flour and cornmeal, then add to butter/egg mixture in three parts. Mix on low speed just until combined.

Evenly distribute batter between the two cake pans.

Bake for about 30 to 45 minutes, until a toothpick comes out clean.

Cool cakes in pan for 15 minutes. Gently turn out onto cooling rack and rest until completely cool.

Once cool, slice each cake into two layers, so you have four layers total. Brush each layer liberally with bourbon.

ORANGE BUTTERCREAM

9 egg yolks
448 grams granulated sugar
112 grams water
560 grams butter, cubed, at room temperature
5 grams vanilla
Zest of *2* medium oranges

Special equipment:
 candy thermometer

(CONTINUED)

177

In a stand mixer using whisk attachment, whip egg yolks on medium speed until thick and light yellow, 5 to 10 minutes.

Meanwhile, combine sugar and water in a saucepan.

Slowly heat sugar mixture to 240 degrees over medium heat.

Remove from heat.

Over medium-low speed, slowly stream the sugar mixture into the egg yolks. Increase speed to medium-high, and mix until room temperature. Continue mixing and add butter, several cubes at a time, until all butter is evenly blended. Add vanilla and orange zest.

CANDIED CHICKEN CRACKLINS

224 grams water
448 grams brown sugar
15 grams salt
Skin of 1 large chicken

Preheat oven to 250 degrees.

Combine water, sugar, and salt in a saucepan and heat over medium heat until sugar and salt are dissolved. Add the chicken skin and simmer for about 5 minutes.

Remove chicken skins from simple syrup and transfer to an oiled wire rack on a sheet pan.

Bake in oven for 1 ½ to 2 hours, until skin is crispy.

Remove from oven and allow to cool completely. Break skins into desired size pieces.

To assemble cake:

Spread Pepper Jam between each layer of the cake. You will only use about half the jam, but save the rest (it's great on basically anything).

Once the layers are in place, ice the cake with the buttercream until you're satisfied with the way it looks. Once again, depending on your tastes, you may not use all the buttercream (I only used about half). Sprinkle the cake all over with crushed up chicken cracklins.

Frederic Remington
American, 1861 – 1909
The Bronco Buster
c. 1900 – 1909
Bronze
Purchased with funds from the
Morton R. Hirschberg Bequest
AP.1982.2.1

Frederic Remington had already received fame for
his paintings and illustrations of western subjects
before he ventured into sculpture. The Bronco
Buster, *his first three-dimensional work, is also*
one of his best-known pieces. Inspired by one of
his illustrations in Harper's Weekly, *the sculpture*
captures the energy of the horse and rider as each
tries to break the other. The sense of movement is
palpable as the horse rears up and the rider quickly
balances in an effort to stay on.

In his piece The Bronco Buster, *Frederic Remington depicts a cowboy being thrown from his horse. Though Remington was mainly influenced by the cowboys of the West, I saw something a little closer to home: the Florida Cracker. Inspired by this piece, and my own ideas of what a Florida Cracker may eat for dessert, I created the Florida Cracker Cake. Cornbread is everyone's classic ideal of what a cowboy eats out on the range, so I chose to make the cake a cornmeal base. The rich history of datil peppers from Northeast Florida, the ever classic bourbon, and a fun take on cracklins round out my idea for the perfect Florida Cracker dessert.*

—*Adam Burnett*
The Bronco Buster

The Tempest

PRESERVED LEMON RISOTTO WITH KALE AND ANCHO-DUSTED SHRIMP

Steven Gaynor **BISCOTTI'S**

Serves 4 – 6

PRESERVED LEMON

5 lemons, quartered
¼ *cup* salt
Cinnamon, clove, bay leaf, coriander seeds,
  black peppercorns *(optional)*

Coat lemon quarters with salt and re-assemble the lemons to their original form. Pack into a mason jar, layering additional salt and optional spices between the lemons. Fill jar to within one inch of the top of the jar, adding lemon juice if necessary to cover the lemons.

Seal jar and let stand in a warm place for 30 days, shaking the jar every other day to distribute the juices. Preserved lemons will keep for 1 year after opening, with no need to refrigerate.

To use the lemons, strain the juice and rinse the lemons under cold running water.

TOMATO CONCASSE

4 Roma tomatoes
2 *cups* boiling water
2 *cups* ice water

Score the tomatoes and lower into boiling water. Blanch for 15 to 20 seconds, then remove tomatoes to an ice bath. Peel skins, squeeze out seeds, and chop tomatoes.

RISOTTO

¼ *cup* extra virgin olive oil
1 *cup* diced white onion
¼ *cup* minced shallots
1 ½ *cups* Arborio rice
½ *cup* white wine
5 *cups* warm vegetable stock
1 *cup* beech mushrooms
½ *cup* Tomato Concasse
2 *cups* baby kale
Pinch lemon zest
¾ *cup* finely diced Preserved Lemons
4 *tablespoons* salted butter, cold
1 dozen shrimp, butterflied and seasoned with
  ground ancho
Salt and pepper

Heat olive oil in a heavy bottomed pot over medium heat. Sweat onions and shallots in olive oil for 8 minutes. Add rice and stir to coat with oil. Add white wine and stir constantly for 2 minutes, then add half the stock, stirring until liquid is absorbed. Repeat until all stock is absorbed and the risotto is soft and tender, approximately 25 minutes.

Add all of the beech mushrooms and half the tomatoes, kale, zest, and preserved lemons (reserve the other half of ingredients for garnish). Simmer for two minutes then stir in the butter. Season with salt and pepper, to taste.

Meanwhile, grill shrimp and remaining kale. Serve risotto topped with grilled shrimp and kale, and garnish with remaining tomatoes, lemon zest, and preserved lemons.

Bob Thompson
American, 1937 – 1966
The Tempest
1965
Oil on canvas
Purchased with funds from the
Mae W. Schultz Charitable Lead Trust
AP.2011.4.1

African American artist Bob Thompson's vibrantly-colored, abstracted paintings inspired by Old Master scenes garnered the young artist early acclaim. In The Tempest, *he reimagined a painting of the same name by Renaissance artist Giorgione (c. 1477 – 1510). The earlier work has been the subject of much debate throughout the centuries, namely due to its odd composition, which features a fully-dressed man watching a nude woman breastfeeding an infant outside on a hill prior to an impending storm. Thompson's version also leaves unanswered questions about the meaning of the scene, but with its shock of color and gestural shapes, it functions as an independent work rather than merely a recreation of an earlier painting.*

When relating another artist's image to a plate concept, the influences are of course on color and texture. Less obvious are the feelings the image brings to the viewer, and that influence on taste.

In the case of The Tempest, *the colors are vivid and speak for themselves. The textures in my mind are coarse, loose, and almost abstract. For me, the feeling or impression being that nature, the earth, and the sky are vibrant yet at the same time restless and a little foreboding. Therefore the taste should be bright, bold, and earthy, with a hint of something on the back palate.*

On the plate, bright is achieved with preserved lemon and tomato. Earthy is the kale and mushroom, and foreboding is the streak of flavor a hint of ancho brings to the plate and palate.

—Steven Gaynor

The Tempest

The Lake

SKATE (BEET + PALM + RAISIN + "WEEDS")

Daven Wardynski **OMNI AMELIA ISLAND PLANTATION**

Serves 4

PICKLED HEARTS OF PALM

2 – 6-inch sections hearts of palm, sliced into
  ½-inch rings, heart popped out of middle
2 cups rice wine vinegar
1 cup sugar
¼ teaspoon red chili flakes
2 cloves garlic, minced
2 teaspoons thyme, chopped

Simmer all ingredients in a small saucepan for
10 minutes. Remove from heat and allow
to marry for an additional 20 minutes or
overnight.

GOLDEN BEET PUREE

½ pound golden beets, peeled and diced
1 cup white balsamic vinegar
4 tablespoons butter
1 teaspoon kosher salt
¼ teaspoon white ground pepper

Place all beets, vinegar, and 2 cups water in a
small pot and simmer until beets are tender.
Remove the beets from the pot and place in
a blender with ¼ cup of the braising liquid.
Puree until smooth with the butter, salt, and
pepper.

GOLDEN RAISIN PESTO

4 tablespoons lemon oil
¼ cup pine nuts, toasted and chopped
½ cup golden raisins, chopped
½ cup parsley, chopped
¼ cup Parmesan cheese, chopped
1 tablespoon lemon zest, chopped
1 teaspoon capers, chopped
1 tablespoon rosemary, chopped

Fold all ingredients together.

To serve:

4 – 5 ounce skate fillets, cleaned
¼ cup all-purpose flour
1 tablespoon canola oil
Salt and white pepper
Lemon oil
Red-veined wild wood sorrel and celery,
  to garnish

Season the fish with salt and white pepper.
Dust the skate with flour and saute over
medium-high heat until golden brown. Flip
and cook an additional 2 minutes.

Place the 2 tablespoons golden beet puree on
the bottom of each plate. Place fish atop the
beet puree and garnish with pickled hearts
of palm and golden raisin pesto. Add garnish
of picked wild wood sorrel and celery. Finish
plate with a drizzle of lemon oil.

William Glackens
American, 1870 – 1938
The Lake
c. 1913 – 1918
Oil on canvas
Purchased with funds
from the Cummer Council
A.P.1987.2.1

William Glackens began his artistic career as an illustrator for several Philadelphia-area newspapers. In the evenings, he attended the Pennsylvania Academy of the Fine Arts, where he met fellow artist, Robert Henri (1865 – 1929). Glackens and Henri, along with Glackens' high school friend John Sloan (1871 – 1951) and five other artists formed The Eight, a group committed to depicting the realities of urban life. Glackens ultimately broadened his scope to include representations of the leisurely pursuits of the middle class. The Lake depicts a view from New Hampshire's White Mountains, where Glackens and his family spent several summers. It features bright colors and loose brushstrokes, and reflects Glackens' 1912 exposure to contemporary French painting as a buyer for noted collector Albert Barnes (1872 – 1951), founder of Philadelphia's Barnes Collection.

Being born and raised in Michigan, a state that houses over 11,000 inland lakes, I was never more than six miles from one of them. William Glackens paints a small lake in the White Mountains of New Hampshire, which appeals to my Midwest farm boy heritage and eternal love affair with the lake, river, and ocean. My current state of mind is that of Florida, Amelia Island, and the salt marsh—embracing the environment that surrounds me daily.

Some influences on my skate dish are direct, such as the literal translation of fish to The Lake. *Skate, or ray, being one of the most underutilized and delicate flavors, was a natural fit to blend the local waters with this surreal view of life. Others, like the pull of golden beet puree, seemingly mimic the long brush strokes scattered throughout this early 1900s imagery.*

I see earth, water, nature, and organics. Pine trees that teem with the visual of fresh Florida palms are represented in both the poached hearts of palm and in the piney rosemary that is blended into the golden raisin pesto. The fluid golden beet puree is a depiction of the rolling waves of the water as it cascades to your palate. The red-veined wood sorrel are the wild weeds that roll over the ridges, our Amelia Island, and the finished plate. The plumped earthy golden raisins in the pesto are soft, smooth pebbles bursting with sweetness that erupt with the tones of lemon at the base of the water's edge. My use of lemon oil to enhance the overall mouthfeel is created as my final touch, on my canvas, in the same fashion of Mr. Glackens' oil on canvas.

—*Daven Wardynski*
The Lake

Thomas Hart Benton
American, 1889 – 1975
June Morning
1945
Oil on Masonite
Purchased with funds from the Cummer Council, the
Morton R. Hirschberg Bequest, and the Mae W. Schultz
Charitable Lead Trust
AP.1994.2.1

Born in Missouri, Thomas Hart Benton was a leading figure in the Regionalist movement, in which some artists sought to counter the rise of abstract art by highlighting the American experience in rural or small towns. Regionalism, or American scene painting, would be disseminated throughout the country during the Great Depression through the creation of public murals and other works commissioned by the Works Progress Administration.

June Morning, painted after the end of the European conflict of World War II, represents Benton's optimism about the strength of the American psyche. As the dark clouds part to reveal a clear sky, life returns to normal. New flowers and vines take over the broken fence, supplanting the dead tree in the middle of the composition. As Benton's neighbor milks a cow, a calm Atlantic Ocean can be seen in the distance in this view from his mother's property on Martha's Vineyard.

June Morning

BUTTER POACHED MAINE LOBSTER WITH SAGE PESTO, RICOTTA TORTELLINI,
LOBSTER STUFFED SQUASH BLOSSOMS, AND FARM FRESH VEGETABLES

Matthew Brown **COLLAGE**

Serves 1

BUTTER POACHED MAINE LOBSTER

1 – ¾ pound live Maine lobster
2 tablespoons water
½ cup cold salted butter (1 stick), cut into 1 tablespoon chunks

Bring a large pot of water to boil. Turn off heat and add the lobster. Cover with lid and let cook for 3 minutes then remove with tongs and allow the lobster to cool slightly on a tray.

Using sharp kitchen shears, cut lobster shell all the way down its back. Turn lobster over and cut bottom shell all the way down. Peel off shell and remove meat. Using the back of a heavy spoon crack the lobster claws and remove meat. Then cut out the knuckle meat with kitchen shears and reserve for stuffed squash blossoms.

Bring 1 tablespoon of water to simmer over medium-low heat in a medium saucepan. Whisk in 1 piece of butter. When butter has melted, add another piece. Continue with remaining butter pieces, one at a time. Make sure the mixture does not come to a boil, otherwise the butter will separate.

Keeping the heat on medium-low, add the lobster tails and claws, then cook for 5 minutes, turning the lobster pieces every minute or so. Make sure mixture does not boil. Remove lobster from butter and drain on a paper towel.

RICOTTA TORTELLINI

½ cup ricotta cheese
¼ cup grated Parmesan
1 pinch fresh ground black pepper
1 pinch freshly grated nutmeg
Fresh pasta sheets
1 egg mixed with *½ teaspoon* water

Combine first four ingredients in a bowl.

Using a 3-inch round cookie cutter, cut rounds from pasta sheets.

Place 1 teaspoon ricotta mixture in the center of each round. Brush egg wash on the bottom half of the round and fold over to seal. Fold back around your finger and turn down the edge to form a tortellini. Reserve the leftover ricotta mixture for Lobster-Stuffed Squash Blossoms.

Add the tortellini to a pot of rapidly boiling salted water. Cook for 3 to 5 minutes, or until tortellini float to the surface. Remove to a strainer to drain and reserve.

LOBSTER-STUFFED SQUASH BLOSSOMS

3 squash blossoms
Lobster knuckle meat
Ricotta filling
All-purpose flour
Tempura batter
1 cup vegetable oil

Carefully pull out the stepal from the inside of the squash blossoms. Stuff each blossom with lobster knuckle meat and ricotta mixture (the amount you will be able to put in each blossom will depend on the size of the blossoms) then twist the ends to seal in the stuffing.

Dredge the stuffed blossoms in flour then dip in tempura batter.

In a small saucepan, heat vegetable oil to 350 degrees and fry blossoms for one minute on each side. Drain on paper towels and set aside.

SAGE PESTO

3 cloves garlic, chopped
½ cup roasted walnuts
1 cup fresh sage, loosely packed
1 cup fresh Italian parsley
¼ teaspoon salt
¼ teaspoon black pepper
¼ cup olive oil

Place all ingredients except olive oil in a food processor then blend while slowly pouring in the olive oil. Keep in an air tight container.

FARM FRESH VEGETABLES

1 artichoke heart, cooked
3 shaved zucchini ribbons,
    cut ¼ inch thick, blanched
3 sugar snap peas, blanched
Salt and pepper, to taste

Heat the artichoke heart, zucchini, and snap peas in a sauté pan with butter. Season with salt and pepper.

To plate and serve:

1 tablespoon Sage Pesto
3 Ricotta Tortellini
3 Lobster-Stuffed Squash Blossoms
Farm Fresh Vegetables
Butter Poached Maine Lobster
2 nasturtium flowers

Place one tablespoon of pesto onto plate then swipe across plate with the back of a spoon. Place tortellini on top of pesto about one inch apart. Lean each stuffed squash blossom on tortellini. Shingle the artichoke, zucchini, and snap peas throughout the dish. Slice the lobster tail into ½ inch thick slices and lean on the vegetables. Garnish with lobster claw and nasturtium flowers.

"

While crafting this dish, I was inspired by Thomas Hart Benton's June
Morning. *As a painting of a farm on the coast of Martha's Vineyard,
I wanted to create a dish that perfectly showcased the farm-fresh ingredients
you could truly get in the month of June from the local produce market.
Among my selections are sugar snap peas, zucchini, and artichokes. I used
a sage pesto swipe across the plate to represent the sweeping color of the
landscape. My barigoule artichoke and squash blossom were spurred by the
thistle plant in the foreground. The neighbor milking the cow, reminiscent
of fresh cheese, instantly inspired me to make fresh ricotta-stuffed tortellini.
I used edible nasturtium and fennel flowers to signify the red and pink
blossoms, and to embody the Maine Ocean in the background, what else but
fresh Maine Lobster, buttery and cooked to perfection.*

—Matthew Brown
June Morning

66

I saw this piece and right away it reminded me of fresh spring air. The rocky, grassy mountainscape has a lot of color and breaks in color. There are what appear to be goats at the top of the mountainside and a beautiful blue sky with just a tiny puff of cloud. I tried to take the colors and peace that were in this painting and translate them to a theme and color scheme on a plate. Grilled ramp buttermilk and goat cheese also reflect the idea of fresh cheeses and dairy being a large part of spring. All of the green, with budding flowers providing a break in color along with chunks and scrapes of angled rock, make for a beautiful image. The very blue sky just adds to the overall positive feeling of the painting.

—*Edwin Baltzley*
In the Alps

John Singer Sargent
American, 1856 – 1925
In the Alps
1911
Oil on canvas
Purchased with funds
from the Cummer Council
AP.1990.20.1
(detail)

*Although John Singer Sargent was American,
he spent most of his life abroad. His artistic
training encouraged rapid painting rather than the
execution of countless studies, and this expressive
canvas showcases Sargent's quick brushstrokes.
Painted in the Simplon Pass in the Oberland Alps
of Switzerland, this painting's rocks and flowers
emerge from its thick texture. Having gained fame
as a portraitist, Sargent was able to suspend new
portrait commissions after 1907 and devote his
time to watercolors and landscapes.*

In the Alps

CAST IRON ROASTED FLOUNDER, FARRO PICCOLO, GRILLED RAMP BUTTERMILK, GOAT CHEESE, CHARRED OKRA, AND CRUMBLED CORNBREAD

Edwin Baltzley **PALM VALLEY FISH CAMP**

Serves 4

FARRO

3 cups dried farro piccolo
3 tablespoons salt
1 tablespoon unsalted butter

Bring one gallon of water to a boil and add salt. Add the farro and allow grains to boil for about 30 minutes, until tender. Strain through a colander, transfer to a mixing bowl and add butter.

GRILLED RAMP BUTTERMILK

6 to 7 wild ramps
Olive oil
1 ½ cups buttermilk
¼ cup sour cream
2 sprigs dill
Salt

Preheat grill (or skillet if no grill is available).

Thoroughly wash and dry the ramps. Lightly toss in olive oil and salt. Cook ramps on a medium-hot zone on the grill until tender and charred in spots. Transfer to cookie sheet to cool.

Once ramps are cooled, place in a blender with buttermilk, sour cream, and dill. Blend until smooth.

CORNBREAD

You will have plenty of cornbread left over for snacking!

2 cups coarse yellow cornmeal,
    preferably Anson Mills
½ tablespoon baking powder
1 teaspoon baking soda
1 tablespoon salt
3 tablespoons granulated sugar
2 eggs
2 cups buttermilk
½ cup melted butter + *1 knob* for the skillet

Preheat oven to 375 degrees and heat an 8- to 10-inch cast iron skillet on the stove over medium heat.

Place cornmeal, baking powder, baking soda, salt, and sugar in a medium mixing bowl. Whisk in eggs, buttermilk, and melted butter.

Melt the knob of butter in the hot skillet and turn to coat the pan. Pour the cornbread mixture into the skillet and bake for 20 to 30 minutes.

ROASTED FLOUNDER

4 – 7 ounce flounder filets, bloodline removed
4 tablespoons pomace olive oil
Knob of butter
4 tablespoons bacon fat
1 quart fresh whole okra, sliced on a bias
    ¼-inch thick
1 pint local grape tomatoes, cut in half
Salt and freshly cracked black pepper, to taste

Pat flounder dry and season with salt and pepper. Heat a cast iron skillet over medium-high heat. Add oil to the skillet and sear fish until golden brown. Flip fish and add a knob of butter to the skillet. Baste fish with butter until barely cooked through. Remove fish to a plate to rest and wipe the cast iron skillet clean.

Heat bacon fat in the same skillet. Sear okra on the cut sides and add the tomatoes once okra is getting a little color. Season to taste with salt and pepper.

To serve:

4 ounces fresh goat cheese
Fresh micro or baby greens, to garnish

Pour a generous puddle of ramp buttermilk on four plates. Scoop warm farro over buttermilk and place okra and tomato around the farro. Lay fish atop the farro and gently crumble goat cheese and cornbread around the plate. Finish with baby greens and serve.

Dancing Pears II: Fandango

SOUR BEER POACHED PEARS WITH BLACK WALNUT DOUBLE CREAM

Chason Spencer **HOPTINGER**

Serves 3

SOUR BEER POACHED PEARS

3 Bosc pears, whole
2 ½ *cups* Duchess de Bourguignon beer
¾ *cup* granulated sugar
6 brown cardamom pods
2 Vietnamese cinnamon sticks
2 *teaspoons* vanilla extract
½ *tablespoon* salt

Peel pears, leaving the stems attached.

Cut a flat base on each pear and core out the center of each to remove the seeds and create a ping pong ball-sized cavity for the cheese.

Place pears along with the rest of the ingredients in a medium pot and bring to a light simmer. Simmer for 40 minutes on medium-low heat, flipping pears every ten minutes so that all sides cook evenly. Once pears have cooked, remove and cool on a rack.

Continue reducing poaching liquid for approximately 20 minutes, until the syrup coats the back of a spoon. Strain syrup and reserve at room temperature.

BLACK WALNUT DOUBLE CREAM

¾ *cup* Fromage d' Affinois cheese
1 *teaspoon* black walnut bitters

While cheese is cold, fold in black walnut bitters until fully incorporated. Reserve in refrigerator until ready to assemble.

To assemble:

Sour Beer Poached Pears, cooled
Black Walnut Double Cream
9 spring roll wrappers

Preheat oven to 375 degrees.

Place approximately 3 tablespoons of double cream in each pear cavity. Place one spring roll wrapper on the base of each pear and pull leftover wrapper up towards top of pear. Lay two more wrappers around the upper half of each pear.

Bake 10 minutes until wrappers are golden crisp. Serve with syrup.

66

My reasoning for creating this dish was to do my own interpretation of the

original artist's work. When I did my background research on the artist

I found out he liked to focus on detail and simplicity, which is what I focus

on when I create new recipes. Traditionally, pears are poached in red wine,

but since I now work at a biergarten, I chose to go with beer in its place.

I played around with different types of doughs to replicate the painting but

found that spring roll wrappers had the best texture and visual appeal. As

soon as I saw this painting, I was instantly inspired and knew this is the one

I wanted to create a dish around. I only hope now, if the artist were to go back

and look at my dish, he would be proud to see my interpretation of his work.

—*Chason Spencer*
Dancing Pears II: Fandango

Joseph Jeffers Dodge
American, 1917 – 1997
Dancing Pears II: Fandango
1992
Oil on canvas
Gift of Joseph Jeffers Dodge
AG.1996.2.59

Joseph Jeffers Dodge found his inspiration for Dancing Pears *in the ubiquitous wrapped pears from mail order retailer Harry & David. After removing the pears from the refrigerator, he was captivated by the way the paper clung to the fruit. The implied movement of the paper as it unfurls is reinforced by the subtitle* Fandango, *which refers to an upbeat Spanish dance.*

The 1920's...The Migrants Arrive and Cast Their Ballots

BBQ ALLIGATOR RIBS, CAROLINA GOLD RICE PORRIDGE,
BLISTERED BRUSSELS SPROUTS AND PADRON PEPPERS, FLORIDA CITRUS

Kenny Gilbert **GILBERT'S UNDERGROUND KITCHEN**

Serves 4

ALLIGATOR RIBS

¼ *cup* Raging Cajun Spice
   (can be purchased at Gilbert's
   Underground Kitchen)
½ *cup* vegetable oil
1 *tablespoon* kosher salt
4 – 10 *ounce* alligator ribs
2 *cups* chicken broth

Combine Raging Cajun Spice, oil, and salt in
a bowl and mix well. Rub spice mixture onto
alligator ribs and marinate for at least 30
minutes, preferably overnight.

Preheat smoker and regulate to a temperature
of 250 to 300 Fahrenheit.

Place alligator ribs in smoker and cook for
1 hour. Remove from smoker and place in a
baking pan. Add chicken broth and cover pan
tightly with foil.

Bake in a preheated 350 degree oven for
45 minutes.

Remove and allow to cool slightly. Pull meat
into large chunks, removing and discarding
the bones. Reserve meat and keep warm.

CAROLINA GOLD RICE PORRIDGE

1 *quart* water
¼ *cup* butter
2 *teaspoon* kosher salt
1 *cup* Anson Mills Carolina Gold Rice Grits

Combine water, butter, and salt in a medium
pot and bring to a boil. Add grits to pot and
reduce to a simmer. Stirring occasionally, cook
until liquid is gone and consistency is that of
oatmeal/grits texture. Keep warm until ready
to serve.

FLORIDA CITRUS MOP

½ *cup* apple cider vinegar
2 *tablespoons* orange marmalade
2 *tablespoons* sliced scallions on the bias
¼ *teaspoon* crushed red pepper flakes
¼ *teaspoon* black pepper
2 *tablespoons* sliced garlic
⅓ *cups* water
1 *teaspoons* kosher salt

Combine all ingredients and mix together
well.

BLISTERED BRUSSELS SPROUTS AND PADRON PEPPERS

1 *cup* quartered Brussels sprouts
½ *cup* padron peppers, stemmed and cut into
   thirds
Salt and pepper, to taste

Preheat a small fryer to 350 degrees.

Fry Brussels sprouts and peppers until golden
brown. Remove and drain on a paper towel and
season with salt and pepper. Keep warm until
ready to use.

To serve:

Carolina Gold Rice Porridge
Pulled Alligator Rib meat
Blistered Brussels Sprouts and Padron Peppers
Florida Citrus Mop
4 *tablespoons* scallions, sliced on the bias

Place about a cup of rice porridge in the
bottom of a bowl. Top with ¾ cup alligator
meat, about ½ cup brussels sprouts, and
padron peppers. Drizzle 2 tablespoons Florida
citrus mop around the dish and garnish with a
tablespoon of scallions.

Jacob Lawrence
American, 1917 – 2000
**The 1920's...The Migrants Arrive and Cast
Their Ballots** from the Kent Bicentennial Portfolio,
Spirit of Independence
1974
Published by Lorillard, 1975
Serigraph on paper, ed. 44/125
Gift of the Lorillard Corporation
AG.1976.1.8

*In 1941, African American artist Jacob Lawrence
unveiled* The Migration of the Negro, *a group of
60 paintings that traced the vast relocation of
African Americans from the South as they sought
new opportunities and more freedoms in northern
states. The series launched Lawrence's career. In
the early 1970s, the Kent Bicentennial Portfolio
committee asked 12 American artists to create
images that reflected their personal definition of
independence. Lawrence's submission,* The 1920's...
The Migrants Arrive and Cast their Ballot, *shows a
diverse group of African Americans exercising their
rights to vote. Men and women, young and old,
wait for their turn at the voting machine, seen in
the back of the composition.*

"

I am very inspired by Jacob Lawrence's work. Today's struggle is just as relevant as it was during the civil rights movement in Selma, Alabama. I personally felt a connection from South Carolina to North Florida. My dish is a merger between the state of South Carolina and North Florida. Overall I feel that the fight for equality is still real and Underground Kitchen will do its part to provide a place of safety, comfort, and peace for all.

—Kenny Gilbert
The 1920's...The Migrants
Arrive and Cast Their Ballots

Eugène Louis Charvot
French, 1847 – 1924
View of Rue El-Alfahouine
1889
Oil on canvas
Gift of Yvonne Charvot Barnett in memory of her
father Eugène Louis Charvot
AG.1999.5.3

*A distinguished physician and surgeon, Eugène
Louis Charvot served as a military doctor in French
Tunisia and Algeria beginning in 1885. Enthralled
with these new places, he created a large body of
paintings, prints, and watercolors. He wrote to a
niece, "The city of Tunis and particularly the Arab
markets are from the point of view of the artist
beyond all description... all is bright and colored,
luminous and fresh. The cube-shaped houses, the
mosques, dabbled high and low with white lime,
shine under the eastern sun like immense blocks
of chalk."[3]*

View of Rue El-Alfahouine

GRILLED LAMB PATTIES, MEDITERRANEAN SALAD, CHICKPEA PUREE, TZATZIKI SAUCE

Sam Efron **TAVERNA**

Serves 4

LAMB PATTIES

1 pound ground lamb
Dash ground cumin
Dash onion powder
Dash garlic powder
Salt and pepper, to taste

Divide lamb into eight patties, or whatever size you prefer. Season lamb patties with a light dusting of cumin powder, onion powder, garlic powder, salt, and pepper. Grill or pan sear to desired temperature.

MEDITERRANEAN SALAD

½ cucumber, finely diced
2 Roma tomatoes, finely diced
½ red bell pepper, finely diced
½ green bell pepper, finely diced
½ red onion, finely diced
½ *cup* extra virgin olive oil
¼ *cup* red wine vinegar
Zest and juice of 1 lemon
½ *teaspoon* minced garlic
1 *bunch* fresh parsley, chopped
Other herbs, as desired (oregano, chives, and thyme all work -
  preferably fresh but dry work as well)
Salt and pepper, to taste

Combine all ingredients in a bowl and mix well. Season with salt and pepper.

TZATZIKI SAUCE

½ cucumber (use the other half from the Mediterranean salad)
1 *cup* Greek yogurt
Zest and juice of 1 lemon
¼ *teaspoon* ground cumin
¼ *teaspoon* onion powder
¼ *teaspoon* garlic powder
Minced chives
Minced mint
Salt and pepper, to taste

Using the blade attachment on a mandolin, slice cucumber into thin strips. Cut strips into a very fine dice.

Combine all ingredients together in a bowl.

CHICKPEA PUREE

1 *pint* cooked chickpeas
2 *tablespoons* lemon juice
¼ *cup* olive oil
½ *teaspoon* ground cumin
Salt and pepper

Place chickpeas in a blender and add enough water (about ½ cup) to blend to a smooth consistency. Add lemon juice, olive oil, cumin, salt, and pepper, to taste. Blend until all ingredients are well incorporated.

To serve:

Spoon a bed of chickpea puree onto a plate or platter. Top with lamb patties then spoon Mediterranean salad over the lamb. Serve with tzatziki sauce.

I chose this painting because I feel that it conveys a strong sense of place. The perspective invites the viewer to wander down the street and explore the city. Eugène Charvot's style gives the entire piece movement and life. I found it easy to imagine the scene filled with the sounds and smells of this part of the world. From Morocco, Tunisia, Israel, and Turkey, to Greece, Italy, France, and Spain, the flavors of the Mediterranean are as vast as its cultures and rich with history. This is some of my favorite style of food to prepare and I have fond memories of traveling through some of these countries and walking through the streets and markets. At first glance of Charvot's work, I started to think of the smells of grilled lamb with cumin, garlic, and other spices that may fill the air if I was walking down the street in the painting. This recipe is a family favorite in our home. It's delicious, healthy, easy to prepare, and full of Mediterranean flavor.

—Sam Efron

View of Rue El-Alfahouine

66

In this piece I found the feeling of old Florida, with its majestic beauty and ability to humble us in the face of the natural world. We are, at all times, wholly dependent on nature's resources for our survival, and this painting depicts to me both the true dominance of nature over man, and her willingness to share her bounty and beauty. My dish reflects the abundance provided by our region's waters and coastal lands -- fish so fresh one can enjoy it straight from the river, vegetables so flavorful they need little manipulation -- and is a representation of what I would imagine a fisherman's lunch to be on an early spring day.

—Genie McNally
The White Rowboat, St. Johns River

The White Rowboat, St. Johns River

GREEN GAZPACHO WITH QUICK CEVICHE AND JOHNNY CAKES

Genie McNally **THE FLORIDIAN**

Serves 6

GREEN GAZPACHO

For the base:

6 green tomatoes
2 cucumbers, peeled, cored, and roughly chopped
½ *teaspoon* minced ginger
1 ½ *teaspoons* minced garlic
2 *cups* ice water
1 ½ *tablespoons* lime juice
2 *teaspoons* salt (more to taste, after chilled)
2 *teaspoons* chopped oregano
1 ½ *teaspoons* ground coriander
½ *teaspoon* ground cumin
⅓ *teaspoon* allspice
¼ *teaspoon* ground, dehydrated datil pepper (aka Datil Dust)

Preheat oven to 400 degrees.

Core and score green tomatoes and roast in oven for 2 to 3 hours, until soft to the touch.

Combine remaining ingredients in a 4 quart non-reactive stock pot or container. Add roasted green tomatoes and puree with an immersion blender. Alternately, puree in batches in a food processor or blender.

For the "bulk":

1 Vidalia onion, finely chopped
1 poblano pepper, seeded and diced
2 red bell peppers or cubanelle peppers, seeded and diced
3 – 4 golden heirloom tomatoes, chopped; add more if you like your gazpacho chunky
½ *tablespoon* chopped parsley
½ *tablespoon* chopped cilantro
½ *tablespoon* chopped mint
2 green spring onions, finely chopped
2 *ears* corn, cooked and shorn from cob (optional)

Combine all ingredients in a mixing bowl and add to the base while still warm. The heat will help soften the fresh ingredients but will not cook them, allowing them to retain some crunch.

Place assembled gazpacho in a cooler for 2 to 3 hours then check for seasoning. Gazpacho will keep in the refrigerator for 3 to 4 days.

QUICK CEVICHE

1 pound super-fresh flounder (tell your fishmonger you're looking
for "ceviche" grade fish)
4 tablespoons good quality olive oil
6 tablespoons lime juice (about 2 limes' worth)
4 tablespoons Meyer lemon juice (or 3 tablespoons lemon juice and
1 tablespoon orange juice)
2 teaspoons coarse sea salt
2 tablespoons chopped green onions
1 tablespoon chopped parsley
2 teaspoons sugar
½ red onion, frenched (cut into very thin slivers)

Using a sharp, cold knife (keep ice water on hand to dip knife, wipe dry
after each dip), sliver flounder into ¼-inch thin by ½-inch long pieces.

Place fish in a glass baking dish and keep well-chilled as you assemble
the marinade.

To assemble marinade, combine olive oil, lime juice, lemon juice, salt,
green onions, parsley, and sugar in a non-reactive bowl.

Gently toss fish and onions by hand in marinade. Make sure fish is
mostly submerged in marinade and cover bowl tightly with plastic wrap.
Chill one hour then toss fish. Repeat every hour for 3 to 4 hours. By the
end of 4 hours, the fish should be lightly "cooked" through; if you would
like fish more well done, keep in refrigerator overnight.

JOHNNY CAKES, AKA HOE CAKES

Yield: 8 to 12 small cakes

2 tablespoons cold butter, or *2 teaspoons* vegetable oil
2 cups water
½ cup milk or water
1 tablespoon chopped green onions
1 teaspoon salt
1 ½ to 2 tablespoons sugar, to taste
2 cups fine cornmeal or "Quick Grits"

Bring butter, water, milk, green onions, salt, and sugar to a simmer in a
medium saucepan. Remove from heat and whisk in cornmeal; allow to
rest about 5 minutes.

Heat a griddle or pan over high heat. Working in small batches, butter or
oil griddle and ladle on 2 ounce portions (about 4 tablespoons) of batter.
Lower heat to medium-high. The edges of the cakes will start to brown
and you will be able to "scoot" the cakes along the pan when they are
ready to flip; after the first flip, press lightly on the cakes to flatten them
to about ½ inch thickness.

Add oil or butter as needed to keep the griddle well-lubricated. Johnny
cakes should take about 5 to 8 minutes each side. Once cooked, removed
to an oven-safe platter and hold in a low oven until ready to serve.

To serve:

Ladle gazpacho into serving bowls and top each portion with ceviche.
Serve with warm Johnny cakes on the side.

Winslow Homer
American, 1836 – 1910
The White Rowboat, St. Johns River
1890
Watercolor on paper
Bequest of Ninah M. H. Cummer
C.0.154.1

Florida's lush natural beauty appealed to Winslow Homer as both an artist and outdoorsman. He made seven trips to the state, and in 1890 traveled the St. Johns River to fish. During that visit, he was inspired to capture this tranquil scene. Although Florida's dense, exotic landscape would have appeared ominous to some, Homer portrayed a peaceful moment where man and nature coexist in harmony, even while nature's supremacy is asserted through the imposing height of the palm trees.

David Called from his Flock

MILK FED LAMB CARPACCIO, WHITE TOMATO GOAT CHEESE MOUSSE, LAVENDER TOMATO

Matthew Medure **MATTHEW'S**

Serves 6

LAMB CARPACCIO

1 lamb loin, outer fat and sinew removed

Season lamb with salt and pepper. Tear off a generous piece of plastic wrap and place on work surface.

Place lamb on plastic wrap then pull the wrap closest to you over the lamb and roll it away from you. Twist both sides in opposite direction to form lamb into a tight log. Do the same with aluminum foil, then place in freezer overnight.

WHITE TOMATO GOAT CHEESE MOUSSE

Olive oil
2 cups ripe white tomato, halved, seeds removed and diced
2 ounces goat cheese
1 cup heavy cream
4 gelatin sheets
Salt and white pepper, to taste

Heat a heavy bottom saucepot over medium heat. Drizzle a little olive oil in the pot and cook tomatoes until softened, about 10 minutes.

Add cheese and cream, then bring to a gentle simmer. Season with salt and pepper, then transfer to blender. Blend for 30 seconds or until very smooth.

Soften gelatin sheets in cold water for 5 minutes, then gently stir into the tomato mixture. Strain through a fine sieve into a 6-inch square pan. Cover and let set for a couple of hours.

LAVENDER TOMATOES

1 cup local colorful tomatoes, skin and core removed
1 tablespoon extra virgin olive oil
Salt and pepper, to taste
1 teaspoon fresh lavender, minced

Season tomatoes with olive oil, salt, and pepper. Sprinkle with fresh lavender.

PARMESAN CRISP

1 cup Reggiano-Parmigiano, finely grated

Heat a nonstick pan over medium heat. Sprinkle cheese in a narrow rectangle and cook for 1 minute. Remove from pan and allow to harden on work surface.

To serve:

Lamb Carpaccio
White Tomato Goat Cheese Mousse
Lavender Tomatoes
Parmesan Crisp
1 teaspoon curry oil
Lavender, to garnish
Sea salt

Remove the lamb from the freezer. Using a meat slicer, slice very thin, laying out 8 circles per plate. Take a warm spoon to make a cone shape with the mousse and place next to the carpaccio. Place one of each colored tomato on the plate and garnish with cheese crisp, curry oil, lavender, and sea salt.

Carl Andreas Ruthart
German, 1630 – 1703
David Called from his Flock
c. 1672
Oil on canvas
Museum Purchase
AP.1962.2.1

German-born artist Carl Ruthart studied painting throughout Europe, and became well known for his rendering of animals. David Called from his Flock *showcases Ruthart's skill. Taking inspiration from the First Book of Samuel (16:11-13), Ruthart depicted David being summoned to appear before the prophet Samuel, where he will be proclaimed the future king of Israel.*

66

The painting depicts the Biblical story of the Prophet Samuel on a mission from God to appoint David, a sheepherder, as the future king. Lamb, the most revered animal and the most honored food in the Bible, was the visual inspiration to dish up history on a plate as canvas. Deconstructing the components—part of a feast fit for King David—reflects aspects of his life. David's tender heart is the inspiration for the Milk Fed Lamb Carpaccio. The carpaccio represents David's vibrant and colorful season as king. I selected white tomatoes to signify the sacredness of the story. Lavender was the muse for the extravagance of a king's feast. And the goat cheese mousse signifies David's life living in the wilderness among sheep and goats as well as living off the land before his reign as king.

—Matthew Medure
David Called from his Flock

Stream near Giverny

OLIVE OIL POACHED HALIBUT WITH SAFFRON MUSSEL CONSOMMÉ

Scott Schwartz **29 SOUTH**

Serves 4

OLIVE OIL POACHED HALIBUT

4 – 5 ounce halibut filets, skin removed
⅓ cup olive oil
Salt and pepper
Fennel pollen
Finishing salt, such as Bull's Bay Flake

Pre-heat immersion circulator to 125 degrees Fahrenheit.

Season the halibut with salt and pepper and place in a vacuum seal bag with olive oil. Remove air and seal. If you do not have a vacuum seal machine a zip lock freezer bag will work.

Place halibut in immersion circulator for 15 minutes. Remove fish from the bag. The fish will be very delicate. Season fish with fennel pollen and a little finishing salt.

No circulator method:

Place a stockpot in the sink and fill with hot water from the tap. Adjust the water so that when temped with a kitchen thermometer the water is leaving the tap at 125 to 130 degrees. With the water running into the stock pot and overflowing at that temperature you have created a crude form of circulator that will work well for this application.

SAFFRON MUSSEL CONSOMMÉ

2 tablespoons olive oil
1 onion, thinly sliced
2 cloves garlic, thinly sliced
1 carrot, thinly sliced
2 tomatoes, seeded and chopped
Stems from *1 bunch* parsley
1 ½ pounds unpeeled shrimp, preferably heads on
1 pound mussels
10 cups water
2 teaspoons saffron threads
2 ½ teaspoons salt
Generous grinding of black pepper
3 egg whites

Heat the oil in a medium stockpot over low heat. Add onion, garlic, carrot, tomatoes, and parsley stems and cook, covered, until soft, about 10 minutes. Stir from time to time to keep vegetables from sticking to bottom of pot.

Add the shrimp and mussels and stir to coat with other ingredients. Add the water, saffron, salt, and pepper. Bring to a simmer over medium-high heat; as soon as gentle bubbles form on the surface, reduce the heat to low. Cook 35 minutes.

Drain the stock through a strainer, then cover and refrigerate the liquid until cool. Reserve about ¼ pound of the cooked shrimp and refrigerate. Discard the remaining solids.

To clarify the consommé, remove the broth from the refrigerator and discard the fat on the surface. Heat the broth in a large saucepan or small stockpot over medium-low heat. While the broth is warming, shell the reserved cooked shrimp and put the meat in the food processor. Add the egg whites and puree until you have a light pink foam, about 30 seconds.

Whisk the shrimp mixture into the broth and continue to heat, whisking steadily until it boils, then reduce the heat to a simmer. Keep whisking slowly but constantly. After about 30 minutes, small bits of egg white will begin to accumulate into larger pieces, about the size and shape of snowflakes. Stop whisking and let the mixture continue to heat. The egg white bits will eventually collect into a moist "cap" on top of the broth. Poke a hole in the center with a spoon to allow the broth to bubble without overflowing. The broth should be in constant gentle motion, not boiling hard. Cook 1 hour without stirring.

Using a slotted spoon or Chinese wire skimmer, very gently lift the cap from the broth and discard. Ladle the broth into a fine-mesh chinois; otherwise, line a strainer or colander with moistened paper coffee filters. Pour the broth gently, ladling the liquid against the sides of the strainer and moving from spot to spot to avoid pushing any egg white through into the consommé. The finished consommé should be completely clear. If it is still cloudy, repeat the clarification process. If the flavor lacks intensity, reduce the consommé over high heat 5 to 10 minutes.

To serve:

Squash blossom
Long stem artichoke, cooked and halved
Blue violas
Micro mustard cress
Micro potato, cooked
Baby tomato, peeled
4 ounce mini pitchers with hot consommé

In a wide, shallow pasta bowl or coupe dish, place a squash blossom and half of an artichoke in the center. Top with a piece of fish. Garnish the plate around the fish with the flowers, cress, potato, and tomato. At the table, gently pour hot consommé around the fish.

"

Frieseke was an impressionist artist who was fascinated by the study of light and particularly how sunshine played on the subject of his works. In the painting we see a landscape of the stream and town of Giverny, France. The rich colors one could assume were present were whitewashed by midday sun, creating a pastel palette. It is this whitewashed and delicate palette I have used to create my dish. Using a poached fish and light saffron broth I achieve a similar delicate and whitewashed pastel effect. The garnish plays off of the color scheme with the violas and also grounds the dish in summer. The flavors are simple yet refined and elegant.

—Scott Schwartz
Stream Near Giverny

Frederick Carl Frieseke
American, 1874 – 1939
Stream near Giverny
after 1898
Oil on canvas
Gift from the Collection of Mrs. C. Herman Terry
and the late C. Herman Terry
AG.2006.10.1

American painter Frederick Carl Frieseke spent much of his adult life abroad. While residing in the French village of Giverny, he and his family lived next door to noted Impressionist Claude Monet (1840 – 1926). This painting reflects a lighter palette typical of Impressionist paintings and Frieseke's continued interest in capturing the effects of sunlight.

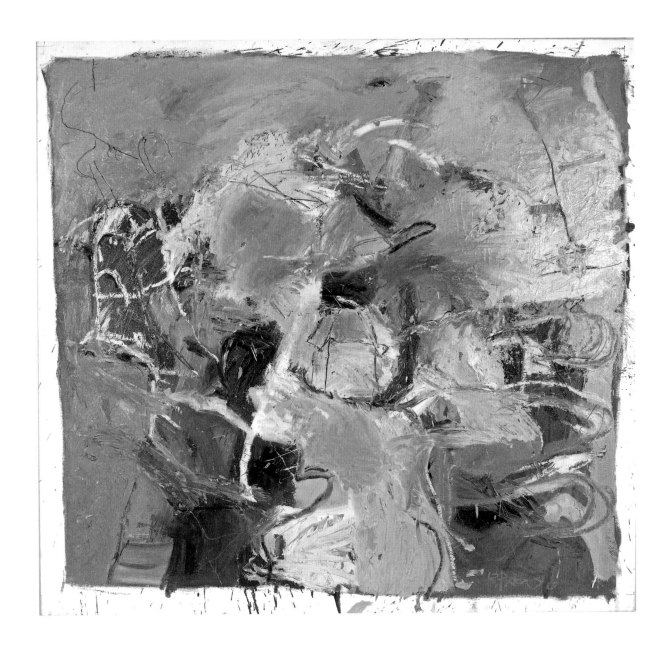

Richard Protovin
American, 1945 – 1991
High Tide
1990 – 1991
Oil on canvas
Gift of Jody Protovin
AG.2006.3.1

Artist and film maker Richard Protovin founded the animation department at New York University's Tisch School of the Arts. In 1988, he moved to Florida's Gulf Coast to work as professor of animation production and cinema studies at the University of Tampa. Protovin described abstract painting as "creating a new order from chaos...like another language...the paintings come from light and memories and discoveries... the strokes, choice of colors, the size – all have to do with some sort of defense and embrace."[4]

66

I chose this painting because it was intriguing and left a lot to the imagination. The title High Tide *and colors reminded me of the ocean and cool water. I took that one step further and envisioned frozen water since the blues and whites of the painting reminded me of a baked Alaska. The red in the painting instantly made me think of raspberries. The wonderful thing about art is the way it can be interpreted.*

—*Michael Bump*
High Tide

High Tide

BAKED ALASKA

Michael Bump **RESTAURANT ORSAY**

Serves 6

CHOCOLATE RASPBERRY BROWNIE

7 ounces whole eggs, beaten
14 ounces sugar
5 ounces all-purpose flour
5 ounces unsweetened cocoa powder
1 teaspoon salt
2 teaspoons vanilla extract
12 ounces unsalted butter, melted and cooled
5 ounces chocolate chips
5 ounces raspberry jam

Preheat oven to 350 degrees. Spray a 9 x 13-inch baking pan with cooking spray.

Mix eggs and sugar together until well blended then add flour, cocoa powder, salt, and vanilla. Add butter and mix until fully incorporated. Fold in chocolate chips.

Pour batter into baking pan. Place raspberry jam in a small zip top bag, cut off a corner and squeeze the jam over the top of the brownie batter.

Bake for 25 to 30 minutes, or until a toothpick inserted in the center of pan comes out clean. Remove from oven and allow brownie to cool completely.

WHITE CHOCOLATE CHIP RASPBERRY ICE CREAM

For ice cream base:

2 cups half and half
½ vanilla bean, scraped
  (or 1 teaspoon vanilla extract in a pinch)
4 cups heavy cream
11 ounces granulated sugar, divided
5 ¾ ounces egg yolks
1 pound good quality white chocolate,
  chopped into small pieces
½ cup dark chocolate shavings or chips

For raspberry sauce:

8 ounces raspberries
6 ounces sugar
1 ounce water

To make ice cream base: Heat the half and half in a pot with the vanilla bean, cream, and half the sugar. Bring to a simmer.

Meanwhile, mix the egg yolks with the remaining sugar.

When the cream has reached a simmer, slowly whisk it into the egg and sugar mixture. Return mixture to the pot and cook over a low to medium heat until it reaches 174 degrees.

Place the white chocolate in a large bowl. Pour the hot base over the chocolate and stir until the chocolate has melted completely. Strain and cool completely.

To make raspberry sauce:

Place raspberries, sugar, and water in a pot and cook over low heat until mixture is syrupy and sugar has completely dissolved. Strain to remove the seeds, then cool and set aside.

To make ice cream:

Place ice cream base in an ice cream machine. Spin the ice cream according to manufacturer's instruction. Right before it comes together, drizzle the raspberry sauce (you don't need to use all of it) into the ice cream and sprinkle in the dark chocolate. Remove ice cream from machine and freeze until ready to assemble baked Alaskas.

MERINGUE

12 ounces granulated sugar
6 egg whites

Add the sugar and egg whites to a double boiler. Cook, stirring, until the sugar has completely dissolved. Remove from double boiler and place in mixing bowl. With whip attachment, whip the whites till glossy and stiff.

To assemble the Baked Alaskas:

Cut brownies into squares or circles. Top brownie with a scoop of ice cream then pipe the meringue all over the ice cream, making sure not to leave any gaps. I prefer to make little "kisses" all over the ice cream.

Torch the meringue with a torch until it caramelizes and serve immediately.

Marie Laurencin
French, 1885 – 1956
Three Dancers
c. 1945
Oil on canvas
Gift of Mr. Jack Bear
AG.1996.4.1

French painter, printmaker, and stage designer Marie Laurencin was actively involved with the French avant-garde movement. Although she was sought out for her high-society portraits, most of her subjects nevertheless resemble the dancers seen here, with large eyes, small noses, and dominant lips.

© Fondation Foujita/Artists Rights Society (ARS), New York/ADAGP, Paris 2015

Three Dancers

GOAT CHEESE TERRINE

Michael Lugo **MICHAEL'S TASTING ROOM**

Serves 4

8 ounce log fresh goat cheese
Red chili flakes, to taste
Heavy cream, if needed
3 tablespoons basil pesto
¼ cup Kalamata olives, pitted and chopped
3 tablespoons sun dried tomatoes, chopped
Salt and pepper, to taste
Extra virgin olive oil
Balsamic reduction
Fresh herbs, chopped
Crackers or crostini, for serving

Remove goat cheese from refrigerator and allow to sit at room temperature for about an hour to soften.

Place softened goat cheese and chili flakes in a food processor and process until smooth. Add a little heavy cream if goat cheese is not mixing well, but not too much or the terrine will not set. Season to taste with salt and pepper.

Line a 2 x 4-inch terrine mold (or small high-sided bowl) with plastic wrap, allowing for three inches of overhang. This will help release the goat cheese terrine from the mold and keep mess to a minimum.

Spread half of the cheese mixture on the bottom of mold. Next, spread the pesto on top of cheese, followed by olives and sun dried tomatoes. Place remaining cheese on top, then smooth and pack down the terrine. Fold plastic wrap over the top of cheese and chill for at least an hour, or overnight.

Unmold terrine by opening plastic wrap and turning over onto a plate. Drizzle with olive oil and balsamic reduction and scatter fresh herbs on top. Serve with crackers or crostini.

Three Dancers *reminded me of one of our most popular dishes at the restaurant. It also plays on the number three. A terrine is layered in threes and our use of ingredients plays beautifully with the dancers' shades in the painting.*

—*Michael Lugo*
Three Dancers

After a Wedding

LIME CHIFFON CAKE WITH BERRY BUTTERCREAM AND TOASTED SWISS MERINGUE

Calli Webb **BREW FIVE POINTS**

LIME CHIFFON CAKE

13 ½ *cups* all-purpose unbleached flour
6 *tablespoons* baking powder
2 *tablespoons* salt
24 egg yolks
6 *tablespoons* vanilla
3 *cups* sugar
Zest and juice of 3 limes
36 egg whites
6 *cups* sugar

Preheat oven to 350 degrees.

In a large bowl, whisk flour, baking powder, and salt together until well combined.

In a separate bowl, whisk together egg yolks, vanilla, sugar, and lime zest and juice. Slowly add wet ingredients to dry ingredients, and then fold together until batter is fully incorporated.

In a stand mixer, beat egg whites on high speed until frothy. Slowly add sugar and continue to beat until stiff peaks form. Fold this meringue into cake batter in thirds until combined and a few white streaks remain.

Divide cake batter evenly between four 12-inch cake pans and three 8-inch cake pans.

Bake for 25 to 30 minutes, or until middle is set and bounces back but does not sink when pressed. Allow cakes to cool completely before frosting.

BERRY BUTTERCREAM

1 *pound* cream cheese, at room temperature
2 *pounds* salted European butter, at room temperature
6 *pounds* powdered sugar
2 *cups* mixed berries (blueberries, raspberries, strawberries)

Beat together cream cheese and butter on medium speed until smooth and fully combined. Slowly add powdered sugar on low speed. Once combined, whip on medium speed and slowly add in berries. Whip for about 2 minutes until frosting is fluffy and berries are incorporated.

Once cakes are completely cool, stack the layers and frost the cake.

TOASTED SWISS MERINGUE

10 egg whites
2 *cups* sugar

Whisk egg whites and sugar together over a double boiler. Heat slowly until sugar dissolves and the mixture is smooth when rubbed between your fingers; there should be no sugar granules.

Pour into mixer fitted with whip attachment and whip on medium-high for about 8 to 10 minutes, or until meringue has formed.

Spread meringue over frosted cake and torch immediately. Decorate cake with foliage.

I'm attracted to the brighter things in life. With the name After a Wedding, *this painting is laced with a backstory that I wanted to recreate. I imagined what the cake would be for the wedding that hosted these bouquets. However, I did not want to paint the cake with roses. Instead, I mixed colors that bring the brightness from the painting to the cake, and incorporated airy wisps to represent the ribbons. With this, I created a cake that has a personality as large as the painting itself.*

—*Calli Webb*
After a Wedding

Janet Fish
American, b. 1938
After a Wedding
2002
Oil on canvas
Purchased with funds from the
Morton R. Hirschberg Bequest and
gifts from the J. Johnson Gallery
AP.2005.9.1

Contemporary realist painter, Janet Fish, creates still life scenes in which the objects themselves are not the primary players. Rather, the colors and light effects create movement throughout the composition. The arrangement of the objects, which often takes several days to finalize, reveals Fish's interest in juxtapositions. Large and small, bright and shadow, heavy and soft combine seamlessly in After a Wedding, *where light dances across vibrant flowers in glass jars, tossing shadows on to a white cloth and colored ribbons that rest on top of a grassy patch.*

Art © Janet Fish/Licensed by VAGA, New York, NY

Meissen Porcelain Manufactory
German, 1710
Pair of Tea Bowls
c. 1756 - 1757
Porcelain
Gift of Miss Constance I. and
Mr. Ralph H. Wark
AG.2000.2.323-324

As the Meissen Porcelain Manufactory gained more success, it looked to broaden its reach outside of Europe. These saucer-less tea bowls were made for the Turkish market around 1756. An Arabic inscription along the rim proclaims, "Ah, how beautiful, may it taste good to the drinker." Below, stylized lotus flower petals in blue, green, and purple are stippled with dots. In later shipments to Turkey, Meissen opted to alter its noted crossed swords logo with pseudo-Chinese characters because they feared their trademark might look too much like the Christian cross for some buyers.

Pair of Tea Bowls

CAST IRON SEARED FILET MIGNON WITH ROASTED POBLANO PEPPER PUREE,
DRAGON FRUIT DATIL PEPPER JELLY, BASIL AND BLACK PEPPER GOAT CHEESE MOUSSE,
ROASTED GOLDEN BEETS, PICKLED RED ONIONS, FRESH DRAGON FRUIT

Jerry Asker **FUNKADELIC FOOD TRUCK**

Serves 4

CAST IRON SEARED FILET

4 filet mignon
Olive oil
Sea salt and freshly ground pepper, to taste

Preheat oven to 500 degrees.

Rub filets with olive oil and season with salt and pepper. Sear in an extremely hot cast iron pan for 3 to 4 minutes on one side. Flip filets and place in oven. Roast until medium-rare.

Remove filets from oven and rest for 6 to 7 minutes. Slice filets through the middle and present rare side up.

ROASTED POBLANO PEPPER PUREE

2 poblano peppers
Olive oil
Kosher salt and freshly ground pepper

Preheat oven to 400 degrees.

Rub peppers with olive oil, salt, and pepper.

Roast peppers until they begin to deflate and char in spots. Place peppers in a sealed zip lock bag to steam for 20 minutes, or until skin is loosened. Peel skin from peppers and remove seeds. Puree peppers in a food processor until smooth.

FRESH DRAGON FRUIT

1 dragon fruit

Cut dragon fruit in half, then peel and cut into chunks. Save scraps for pepper jelly.

DRAGON FRUIT DATIL PEPPER JELLY

Handful of datil peppers, finely chopped
  (add more peppers for spicier jelly)
1 green bell pepper, finely chopped
8 cups sugar
½ cup apple cider vinegar, to taste
¼ cup fresh lemon juice
Dragon fruit puree
2 packages pectin

Place all ingredients except pectin in a large pot. Bring to a hard boil for about 20 minutes, skimming surface occasionally. Add pectin and continue to boil for 10 minutes, until mixture thickens. Remove jelly from heat and cool overnight in refrigerator.

BASIL AND BLACK PEPPER GOAT CHEESE MOUSSE

2 tablespoons sugar
1 cup heavy cream
1 log goat cheese, at room temperature
Fresh basil
Freshly cracked black pepper, to taste

Place a metal mixing bowl in the freezer for 15 minutes.

(CONTINUED)

Remove bowl from freezer and whisk sugar and cream until stiff peaks form. Add goat cheese, basil, and pepper, then whisk to combine.

ROASTED GOLDEN BEETS

Golden beets
Olive oil
A few *sprigs* of fresh thyme
Kosher salt and freshly ground black pepper, to taste

Preheat oven to 300 degrees.

Toss beets with olive oil, thyme, salt, and pepper, then wrap in a foil pouch. Place pouch in a foil-lined metal pan and cook for 2 to 4 hours, depending on size. Beets are ready when a toothpick is inserted with no resistance. Peel and dice beets.

PICKLED RED ONIONS

5 cups red wine vinegar
4 cups apple cider vinegar
5 cups water
6 cups sugar
½ cup pickling spice
1 bay leaf
6 red onions, julienned

Place vinegar, water, sugar, pickling spice, and bay leaf in a large pot and bring mixture to a boil. Boil for 5 minutes, then pour over red onions. Allow to sit overnight.

To serve:

Artfully arrange elements on a plate and serve.

❝

I chose to incorporate several different Meissen porcelain pieces within my dish. From the teapot depicting scenes from Aesop's Fables to the tea bowl with Arabic inscription, this collection is truly exhilarating. My personal favorite touch to the dish I have created is the use of Dragon Fruit which strongly resembles the tea bowl with Arabic Inscription. Also, what better way to represent the Meissen crossed swords than to do so with freshly pickled red onions! It is my desire that you fancy this representation of the Meissen Collection as much as I enjoyed creating it.

—Jerry Asker
Pair of Tea Bowls

Frans Snyders
Flemish, 1579 – 1657
Still Life with Fruit and Flowers
c. 1630
Oil on panel
Purchased with funds from the
Morton R. Hirschberg Bequest
AP.1984.1.1

The popularity of still life scenes in the Netherlands during the 17th century can be partially attributed to the growing merchant class, who sought decorative paintings for their homes. Many still lifes, however, feature religious or moral undertones. This work by Frans Snyders is no exception. Known as a memento mori, or reminder of death, this painting includes objects with multiple meanings. The highly-detailed cut flowers could represent Dutch prosperity as well as the ephemeral nature of life. On the golden chalice at left, the knight may reference "the Christian soldier" while the porcelain bowls nearby highlight trade with Asia. Grapes commonly symbolize the wine from the Eucharist and, therefore, Christ's blood.

Still Life with Fruit and Flowers

HOG & HOMINY : FRUIT & FLOWERS

Kevin Sbraga **SBRAGA & COMPANY**

Serves 4 – 6

3 *pounds* boneless pork shoulder
1 *bunch* thyme
1 *head* garlic, halved
6 *cups* milk
3 *tablespoons* sugar
¼ *teaspoon* turmeric
2 *cups* coarsely ground polenta
3 *tablespoons* butter
3 whole kernel corn in husk
10 baby corn, cut in half
10 seedless red grapes, cut in half
Kosher salt and black pepper
Corn flowers or any other edible flowers,
   for garnish

Preheat oven to 300 degrees.

Place pork shoulder in a roasting pan fitted with a rack. Season with salt and pepper, covering all sides. Place thyme and garlic on top of the roast and cover roasting pan with foil. Place in oven and cook until tender, about 4 hours. Set aside.

Meanwhile, in a medium saucepot, bring milk, 1 tablespoon kosher salt, sugar, and turmeric to a simmer. Slowly add polenta while whisking constantly. Cook for about 45 minutes over low heat, stirring occasionally to prevent sticking. When polenta is creamy, stir in butter right before serving.

Raise oven temperature to 400 degrees when pork shoulder is finished and resting. Place whole corn, husk and all, on a baking sheet and roast until tender and charred on the outside, about 20 minutes. Allow to cool. Remove husks, cut kernels off the cob and fold into polenta. Set aside.

Toss the baby corn with oil and season with salt before placing on a baking sheet and roasting in the oven, about 10 minutes. Set aside.

Carefully place grapes cut side down on a hot cast iron skillet. Char for about 2 minutes or until grape releases from pan.

To assemble, spoon a cup of polenta in the center of a large bowl. Pull some of the pork off of the roast and place on top. Garnish with baby corn, charred grapes, and edible flowers.

"

Frans Snyders' Still Life with Fruit and Flowers *is beautiful in its simplicity.*
Despite the opulence of the rest of the painting, the fresh fruit and flowers
visually steal the show. This inspired me to play with vibrant colors.
My dish reiterates that we can cook a meat dish that also puts a bounty
of other ingredients front and center, including corn several different ways
and grapes.

We didn't shy away from a straightforward interpretation of using flowers
as a garnish but took it a step further by using corn flowers that grow in the
same fields with the corn we used. To top it off, the charred grapes perfectly
balance the richness of this dish.

—Kevin Sbraga
Still Life with Fruit and Flowers

The Grandchildren of Cousin Shmuel, Copenhagen, Denmark

SUMMER RAVIOLI SALAD

Kathy Collins **NOLA MOCA**

Serves 4 – 6

PASTA DOUGH

3 cups semolina flour
1 cup water
1 teaspoon salt
1 tablespoon olive oil

Mix all ingredients in a stand mixer with dough hook for about 10 minutes. Wrap dough in plastic wrap and let rest at room temperature for 30 minutes.

Make ricotta while dough is resting.

LEMON RICOTTA FILLING

2 quarts whole milk
1 cup heavy cream
½ teaspoon salt
3 tablespoons fresh lemon juice
Zest of 1 lemon
½ tablespoon salt
1 whole egg

Line a large sieve with a layer of cheesecloth and place it over a large bowl.

Slowly bring milk, cream, and salt to a boil in a 6-quart heavy pot over medium heat, stirring occasionally to prevent scorching. Add lemon juice then reduce heat to low and simmer, stirring gently once or twice,

until the mixture curdles, about 2 minutes. Scoop the curds with a slotted spoon into the lined sieve and let it drain 15 minutes. After discarding the liquid, place cheese in a bowl and mix in lemon zest and salt.

Beat egg, fold into cheese and keep chilled.

RAVIOLI

Rested Pasta Dough
Lemon Ricotta Filling
1 cup cornmeal

Bring an 8 quart pot of salted water to a boil.

Divide pasta dough into fourths. Roll one portion to ¹⁄₁₆-inch thickness (about number 6 on a stand mixer pasta roller) and keep the rest of the pasta covered to prevent drying out while you work on each quarter.

Working quickly, place about 1½ tablespoons of filling 4 inches apart over half of a pasta sheet. Use a pastry brush to brush around filling with water to moisten. Fold sheet over and press down to seal. Cut ravioli into circles with a pastry cutter or a large glass. Press around cheese to remove air and seal edges.

Transfer ravioli to cornmeal-dusted sheet pan and cover with a towel so they do not dry out. Repeat until dough and filling are gone.

(CONTINUED)

Cook ravioli in boiling, salted water for 1 to 2 minutes, until they float. Remove with a slotted spoon into an ice bath for 1 minute. Remove ravioli from ice bath and pat completely dry. Transfer to wax paper-lined sheet pan and chill in refrigerator until ready to assemble salad.

KALAMATA OLIVE VINAIGRETTE

½ cup red wine vinegar
1 teaspoon Dijon mustard
1 teaspoon salt
1 teaspoon sugar
1 teaspoon fresh chopped garlic
1 cup olive oil
½ cup Kalamata olives and their juice

Add first five ingredients to blender and start on low, then add olive oil to incorporate and form an emulsion. Add Kalamata olives and juice, then pulse just to break up olives. There should be specks and small chunks of olives. Do not blend completely.

DEHYDRATED OLIVE OIL

4 tablespoons extra virgin olive oil
1 cup tapioca maltodextrin *(available online and in some specialty stores)*
1 teaspoon salt

Add all ingredients to food processor and pulse until olive oil turns into a fine powder, scraping down sides so that all the oil and powder is mixed. If it still seems sticky or not completely dry, add 1 more teaspoon of tapioca maltodextrin until a powder forms, as it can vary by brand.

To assemble:

Lemon Ricotta Ravioli
Olive oil
Baby heirloom tomatoes, tossed in olive oil and sea salt
Grilled asparagus
Pickled baby carrots
Roasted red beets
Kalamata Vinaigrette
Micro arugula, basil, dill, or other herbs and greens
Dehydrated Olive Oil

Place chilled ravioli in the center of the plate and brush with olive oil. Arrange vegetables around ravioli. Drizzle with Kalamata vinaigrette, top with your favorite herbs or greens, and sprinkle with dehydrated olive oil.

Vardi Kahana
Israeli, b. 1959
**The Grandchildren of Cousin Shmuel,
Copenhagen, Denmark**
2004
Archival inkjet print
Gift from the Artist
AG.2014.6.1

*Israeli photojournalist Vardi Kahana spent more than 15 years documenting her family for her series
One Family. Tracing four generations in the years following the Holocaust, her work weaves a complex
narrative of Jewish Israeli society—from her parents and their siblings, all Holocaust survivors, to their
great grandchildren. This photograph shows the grandchildren of her cousin, Shmuel, living in Denmark.
Collectively, the children have grandparents who are Jewish, Christian, and Muslim, but they share a
grandfather who was a survivor of the Holocaust. Kahana describes the three religions on a trampoline
as an image of "hope."*

"

I was immediately drawn to this work because it snapped me back to my childhood in the Chicago area. We had a trampoline and a pool, so I spent the majority of my summers in the backyard. My family's birthdays—my two younger brothers, my mom, and my dad—are all in the summer. So between birthdays and all the summer holidays, my mother spent a lot of time making gigantic Tupperware bowls of pasta salad for our endless outdoor parties. It is a dish that I love, but it has a bad rap because it can be made really carelessly and taste awful. This recipe uses super-fresh ingredients and elevates pasta salad to an amazing first course. Or it can become an entree by adding a few more ravioli, vegetables, and a delicious piece of grilled fish or chicken.

—Kathy Collins
The Grandchildren of Cousin Shmuel,
Copenhagen, Denmark

Keith III

GORGONZOLA-STUFFED BLACK RAVIOLI, RICOTTA SALATA, SQUID INK BALSAMIC REDUCTION

Howard Kirk and Brian Moore **13 GYPSIES**

Serves 4

GORGONZOLA FILLING

1 cup ricotta
1 cup gorgonzola
Salt and pepper

Prepare your filling by mixing the ricotta and gorgonzola. The ricotta will tame the aggressive flavor of the gorgonzola and give it a boost in moisture, which will result in a silkier mouth feel. Using a mixer for this will give you a more homogenized final product, but who cares - this is pasta! Let it be rustic and combine it with your hands or a spoon and a good amount of passion and love. Season to taste with salt and pepper.

PASTA DOUGH

3 cups durum semolina flour
1 cup water
1 ounce squid ink

Combine flour, water, and squid ink in the bowl of a stand mixer with a dough hook. Mix dough until it has formed and has a bouncy texture. Wrap dough in cling film and allow to rest for 30 minutes.

Divide the dough ball into four equal parts and begin to roll it out. If using a rolling pin, roll out gently, spinning the mass every pass until you get the desired thickness you want. If using a mixer pasta attachment, roll on the largest setting once and then roll once on every setting until you reach setting 3. When you reach setting 3, start at the largest setting again, but this time fold the sheet and turn it before you feed it through, passing it through each setting 3 times until you reach setting 4. Whether you use a pasta attachment or roll it out by hand, deciding on your final thickness for ravioli is different than other types of pasta. Remember that the edges of the ravioli will be twice the thickness.

Now to make your ravioli. If you want to re-create this dish verbatim you will need to cut discs out of your pasta sheets using a ring mold or a biscuit cutter. When first starting with no money, we used an empty tin can to cut our ravioli back in the day - and so can you. You will need 2 discs per ravioli. Lay down one disc, spoon in some of the filling (or use a piping bag or cornerless plastic bag), place another disc on top and press out all of the air. Crimp the edges with a fork. If you find that the pasta is not crimping easily, mist the inside of the top disc with a little water before setting it on top of the filling. Set aside.

BALSAMIC GLAZE

1 cup Modena-style balsamic vinegar
4 grams squid ink
Creme fraiche
Ricotta salata, shaved
Pea shoots (optional)

Combine vinegar with squid ink in a small saucepot. Cook to reduce until slightly runnier than syrup. Set aside.

Place the creme fraiche in a pan with a splash of water to loosen it up. Gently cook until the creme fraiche relaxes into the consistency of a sauce. Set aside, but keep warm.

To assemble, boil ravioli in heavily salted water until al dente. Al dente to us might not be al dente to you. Everyone is different. Cook the ravioli until you are happy with it, but be warned that fresh pasta cooks fast. Drain quickly on a paper towel.

Spoon some of the creme fraiche sauce on the bottom of a plate or pasta bowl. Place ravioli on creme fraiche and top with shaved ricotta salata and a drizzle of balsamic squid ink glaze. Garnish with pea shoots, if desired.

We chose Keith III as our inspirational piece because it was simple and complex, bold and quiet, elegant and reserved—but most of all we chose it because we wanted a challenge. Any chef in his right mind is going to choose to work with inspiration that is bright, vibrant, and full of color. Thankfully we are not known for going with the grain. We wanted to push ourselves by picking a beautiful piece that is greyscale. Any decent cook can make a good plate of food if they have the best ingredients and can use any and all of the ingredients they want. A great cook can turn the worst cut of beef into something beautiful, gorgeous, and delicious. I am by no means saying that we are great cooks, but we wanted to push and test ourselves to work within limits. Black and White. We had to create a plate of food that was not only delicious, but had to be beautiful. It had to pay respect to the art that inspired it.

—Howard Kirk and Brian Moore
Keith III

Without the contributions of time, talents, and support from so many, creating this book would have been impossible. We want to extend a very special thank you to all our participants, as well as these cookbook sponsors for their important financial support:

COOKBOOK SPONSOR

Cheney Brothers

COOKBOOK PARTNERS

Buffalo Trace Bourbon
The Candy Apple Café and Cocktails
Community First Credit Union

RESTAURANT SPONSORS

Biscotti's
Black Sheep
The Floridian
Taco Lu

IN-KIND SPONSORS

Agnes Lopez Photography
Varick Rosete Studio

ARACELI AND JAYCEL ADKINS
CELY'S FILIPINO FOOD

Araceli and Jaycel Adkins are the mother/son chefs of Cely's Filipino Food, a Filipino food truck in Jacksonville. Araceli Adkins has been a chef and small business owner for over 25 years in the restaurant industry. Jaycel Adkins is a graduate of the French Culinary Institute and has worked in the family business since he was small. They can be found every Saturday at the Riverside Arts Market and at various events, including One Spark Festival and THE PLAYERS Championship, serving their take on Filipino Street Food.
127–131

MARGIE ASHENS
NORTH BEACH FISH CAMP

A native of Detroit, Michigan, Chef Margie studied at the Culinary Studies Institute at Oakland Community College. She worked under Chef Brian Polcyn at Chimayo and Certified Master Chef Milos Cihelka at the Golden Mushroom before moving to Jacksonville. As a 20-year resident of Jacksonville, Chef Margie has been the Pastry Chef of Giovanni's, the Chef de Cuisine of Marker 32 Restaurant, and she is currently the Chef de Cuisine of the North Beach Fish Camp. She enjoys being a mother and a wife, traveling to find great food, and antique shopping. She also enjoys gardening, but her garden does not enjoy her, as she is cursed with a black thumb. In the culinary arts, she enjoys baking breads and creating pastries.
75–78

JERRY ASKER
FUNKADELIC FOOD TRUCK

Gerald (Jerry) Asker was born and raised in Jacksonville and early on showed a talent for cooking in his parents' restaurant. Throughout his years working at Jerry's Grille, he created his own style of cooking and desired to open a restaurant of his own. His fiancé at the time, Amanda, half-jokingly suggested to open a food truck instead so they could "HIT THE ROAD!" Funkadelic Food Truck was born. Jerry decided to purchase an old Step Van so he would have the ability to build out his mobile kitchen just as he'd envisioned it. After three short months, Funkadelic was ready to hit the streets! Jerry opened his Funk Mobile's window for service in December 2013 and has been going strong ever since.
254–258

EDWIN BALTZLEY
PALM VALLEY FISH CAMP

Chef Edwin Baltzley grew up in the panhandle of Florida. One of his earliest memories is his grandmother teaching him how to throw a cast net to catch blue crab in the local bayous. After moving to Jacksonville in 2005 he met his mentor, Chef Benjamin Groshell, the owner and Chef de Cuisine of Marker 32 Restaurant. After three years at Marker 32, Chef Ed followed his mentor's footsteps to attend the Culinary Institute of America in Hyde Park, New York. While studying at CIA, Chef Ed worked at Park Avenue Restaurant in New York under Chef Craig Koketsu. Chef Ed moved back to Jacksonville in 2011 and reunited with Chef Groshell and Chef Sergio Zucchelli to become the Sous Chef of the Palm Valley Fish Camp. One year later, he became the Chef de Cuisine. Chef Ed has a beautiful wife, two lovely daughters, and a little old house down in St. Augustine. When he's not cooking, he enjoys fishing, reading, and gardening.
201–206

MATTHEW BROWN
COLLAGE

Native Floridian Chef Matthew Brown first discovered his passion in culinary arts as a teenager while traveling throughout Europe. Diving into his career at Stonewood Grill in Jacksonville Beach, he worked his way to head Chef within three years. Later working under Chef Ted Peters at One Ocean, he refined his skills. Now, Executive Chef at both Blackfly and Collage Restaurants in St. Augustine, Matt is the force behind Collage being named one of Top 100 Restaurants in the U.S. by OpenTable. Recently partnering with Hastings Farm Rype & Readi, he proudly builds a menu with fresh, local ingredients.
194–200

MICHAEL BUMP
RESTAURANT ORSAY

Michael Bump graduated from Western Culinary School in 1997. After graduating, he realized his love for pastry while working in Monterey, California. In 2003, he moved to Kansas City where he worked under James Beard award-winning chefs Debbie Gold and Michael Smith. In 2008, he was published in Pastry Arts & Design magazine. Michael was hired as Pastry Chef at Restaurant Orsay when he moved to Jacksonville. After four years, owner Jonathan Insetta opened a sister restaurant, Black Sheep, where Michael is also in charge of the pastry program. Michael took part in the *Cooking with Intuition* cookbook and was a featured chef by Pacojet. Currently you can find Michael in the back of the kitchen at Orsay working on new desserts and ideas. When he is not there, he is hanging out with his family and spending quality time with his son Myles.
241–245

ADAM BURNETT
KNEAD BAKESHOP

Some of my fondest memories from childhood revolve around baking with my Memaw at her house in Auburn, Alabama. Years later, while working at restaurants in Portland, Oregon, I once again fell in love with baking. After going

to Oregon Culinary Institute and working at bakeries in Oregon for several years, I moved back to Florida to make pastries for Bold Bean Coffee. Two years later, I had that itch to expand, and Knead was born. When not working, I like to cook out with friends, read books about food, play with my dog, Newman, and listen to Dolly Parton.
177–182

BLAKE BURNETT
CHEW CHEW FOOD TRUCK

Blake Burnett is chef, owner, and operator of Chew Chew Food Truck. Blake is originally from Bradenton, Florida and has been living in Jacksonville for 12 years. He started working in restaurants at the age of 16 and quickly found a passion for the business. Blake attended the culinary program at Florida State College of Jacksonville, which gave him the opportunity to hone his skills in some of Jacksonville's finest restaurants. His love of food and creative expression, paired with the guidance of some great chefs, gave him the confidence to start Chew Chew Food Truck in September of 2013. Chew Chew is known for its eclectic fare. Blake finds his greatest inspiration for his dishes through traveling, surfing, and eating whatever comes his way.
122–126

ZACK BURNETT
BOLD BEAN COFFEE ROASTERS

Zack Burnett is co-owner and green coffee buyer for Bold Bean Coffee Roasters. In his eight years in the coffee industry, he's created the award-winning Bold Bean Coffee Roasters retail coffee shop model and built its nationally-recognized green coffee buying, roasting, training, and wholesale programs. Zack is the driving force behind Bold Bean's approach of continual development, growth, refinement, and fun. His job routinely takes him to coffee growing regions around the

world in search of the best coffees for Bold Bean customers. Zack dreams of one day owning and operating a coffee farm close to some nice waves, somewhere in Latin America.
61–64

DENNIS CHAN
BLUE BAMBOO

Dennis Chan grew up in Jacksonville, where his family has owned 12 restaurants for the past seven decades. After graduating from the prestigious Culinary Institute of America in Hyde Park, New York, Dennis found himself working with Ming Tsai, from PBS' "Simply Ming." It was the perfect platform for him to apply the classic cooking techniques that he learned in school to the traditional Chinese family restaurant format that he grew up with in Florida. Chef Chan opened Blue Bamboo in his hometown of Jacksonville in 2005. In addition to operating Blue Bamboo, Dennis is an adjunct professor at the local state college, and regularly teaches cooking classes at Blue Bamboo. Chan's first cookbook, *Hip Asian Comfort Food*, was published in 2009.
142–146

JASON CHEN
KAZU

Wen Chen, who goes by the English name Jason, was born in Fuzhuo, China in 1982. Jason left China 15 years ago and moved to New York, where he became an apprentice in a high-end sushi restaurant, learning to create original dishes from one of the best sushi chefs in New York City. In 2002, Jason moved to Connecticut, where he reconnected with childhood friend Ming Chen, who goes by David, in a popular Japanese restaurant. The two moved to Jacksonville in 2013 and opened Kazu, a Japanese restaurant and sushi bar in Mandarin. Kazu is the only Japanese restaurant in Jacksonville that offers a variety of sushi-grade fish from around the world,

and Jason is well known for his spectacular presentations.
167–171

KATHY COLLINS
NOLA MOCA

Originally from Chicago and a graduate of the Le Cordon Bleu School in her native city, Chef Kathy Collins has been with NOLA MOCA since 2005. Serving seasonal foods and creating custom menus for catered events at MOCA Jacksonville gives her intimate knowledge of what clients crave. Appearances on television, charity events, and the Publix Aprons Cooking School keep her involved with the community. Her efforts to find local products, use the freshest possible ingredients, and grow some of her own herbs and vegetables have earned NOLA MOCA a Snail of Approval from Slow Food First Coast.
263–267

MEREDITH COREY-DISCH AND SARAH BOGDANOVITCH
COMMUNITY LOAVES

Meredith moved back to Jacksonville after finishing college in the Appalachians and traveling around Europe working on farms and, fatefully, a rustic sourdough bakery. Gaining experience making bread using traditional methods and ethically-sourced ingredients led her to the conclusion that her environmental studies background could be put to use in the kitchen. Upon returning to her hometown she met a fellow bread baker, Sarah Bogdanovitch, and they have been working together ever since. They now own Community Loaves, their own storefront in historic Murray Hill, where they bake sourdough loaves and sweets five days a week and serve farm-to-table meals in their garden.
53–56

Growing up in a large Cuban family, most of Arielle's younger years were spent in the kitchen peeling plantains and mashing garlic for mojo at the side of her abuelitos. She lost track of her passion until she found herself working under Chef Eric at Pastiche. He reignited Arielle's passion in a way that opened her eyes to a whole new world of cooking. Since then she has spent endless hours mastering her craft. Now, going on four sleepless years later, Arielle happily runs Tapa That with her family in the heart of 5 Points.
137–141

Chris Dickerson completed the prestigious Chef's Apprenticeship program at the Cloister Hotel on Sea Island under legendary chef Franz Buck. He cooked at The Little Nell in Aspen under James Beard Award-winner George Mahaffey and worked for Nobu Matsuhisa. He has been invited to cook with many notable chefs and was part of a team that cooked for Paul Bocuse.
26–29

Chef Sam Efron, a Jacksonville native, developed his culinary style through a combination of formal and experiential training. He discovered European cuisine while living abroad as an exchange student from Florida State University; upon graduation, he enrolled in the Culinary Institute of America. He quickly refined his skills at landmark restaurants such as Four Seasons Hotel New York, Gramercy Tavern, Aqua, and Silks at The Mandarin Oriental Hotel, San Francisco. Upon returning to Jacksonville, Sam assisted in the opening of Restaurant Orsay before he opened Taverna with his wife, Kiley, in 2009. Taverna is a restaurant that draws inspiration from the simplicity and warmth of rustic Italian kitchens. Located in Jacksonville's historic San Marco neighborhood, which was designed to resemble the Piazza di San Marco in Venice, this rustic, yet sophisticated dining destination has earned numerous accolades since opening in 2009.
216–221

Chef Eddy Escriba was born in Guatemala City and is known for his flavorful, humble cooking style, which he attributes to the family-style dinners and traditional Guatemalan dishes he grew up cooking for family and friends. His family relocated to Cleveland, where Chef Eddy finished high school. He studied culinary arts at Florida Culinary and has many successful restaurant ventures in South Florida under his belt. Chef Eddy had always dreamed of opening his own restaurant, and when the opportunity presented itself in Jacksonville, he decided to relocate and open Burrito Gallery. Voted best Burrito in Jacksonville by Folio Weekly, he decided to spread his wings and venture into a new restaurant concept. Uptown Market (now Uptown Kitchen + Bar) was opened, featuring a Southern-style diner concept. Uptown Kitchen + Bar is true to Chef Eddy's vision of using pure simple local ingredients at the peak of season.
30–34

Jamey's love of cooking started as a young child in the kitchen with his grandmother. He went to college on a tennis scholarship and ended up studying business and finance at the University of Florida. However, like most good career paths, his ambition led him down a new road. At the age of 24, he started cooking professionally. His impressive resume includes time spent working under some of the biggest names in the restaurant world, like Louis Chatham of Commander's Palace, and being the Executive Chef of the Four Star and Four Diamond award-winning restaurant Manuel's on 28th. He is now the Executive Chef of The Candy Apple Café and Cocktails, as well as its parent company and associated brands: The Chef's Garden, CG Dinner Club, and the Cummer Café. When he is not cooking in one of his kitchens, he is busy being a dad to his two girls, Charlee and Catye.
15–19, 147–151

Andrew Ferenc, Chef/Owner of On the Fly Sandwiches & Stuff, stands as one of the pioneer's of Jacksonville's food truck scene. Andrew has been working in kitchens since the age of 15 and used his 19 years of experience to create his restaurant on wheels in 2011. His attention to detail, plate presentation, and ability to create eclectic dishes has garnered numerous accolades. Chef Andrew has received "Best of" Awards in Jacksonville Magazine, Folio Weekly, and Void Magazine, and has won multiple Food Truck Champion and People's Choice Titles at the Jax Truckies Food Truck Championships.
105–109

MALLORIE FINNELL
B THE BAKERY FOR BB'S AND BISCOTTI'S

Mallorie Finnell began working in the food industry at age 15. A 2008 graduate of Le Cordon Bleu College of Culinary Arts in Orlando with a degree in Baking and Pastry, she has worked in a variety of bakeshops from mom-and-pop to large-scale commercial operations. During a nearly three-year tenure at Sweet By Holly in Orlando, she worked under the direction of then Kitchen Manager/ Pastry Chef Krista Newman, creating dessert selections for the opening of Martha Stewart and KB Homes Mabel Ridge Community in Orlando, the United Way Chef Gala at Disney's Epcot Center, and the Tim Tebow Foundation, among others. In 2013 she moved to Jacksonville to be Pastry Chef at B the Bakery. She found a home at Biscottis, one of Jacksonville's best-loved restaurants, where her contributions of new desserts and elegant wedding cake designs have made her one of the area's most respected Pastry Chefs.
40–44

STEVEN GAYNOR
BISCOTTI'S

Steven Gaynor grew up on Long Island, spending his youth surf-casting striped bass and spearing flounder. His Spanish grandmother introduced him to cooking with seasonal ingredients and taught him the classic art of creating old-world-style dishes. Chef Steven travelled and worked in the Hamptons and New York City before moving to Melbourne, Florida, where he owned a restaurant for 10 years. Biscottis has flourished as a result of his lifelong passion for rustic cuisine with a Mediterranean influence. From his travels, he has mastered the ability to create any menu a client may desire. Saltimbocca, paella, and of course his signature chicken francaise are favorites on the dinner menu at Biscottis.
185–188

KENNY GILBERT
GILBERT'S UNDERGROUND KITCHEN

Chef Kenny Gilbert is best known for his appearance on "Top Chef" Season seven, where he instantly became one of the most likable cheftestants to date. Throughout his career, Kenny has traveled the world, staging in some of the top restaurants in Japan, Spain, France, and the Caribbean. He has cooked at the James Beard House, participated in wine and food festivals around the country, cooked for the Sports Illustrated Super Bowl party, and appeared on the "Today Show," Jacksonville's FOX 30, and in the LA Times. Kenny has cooked for the likes of Oprah Winfrey, Gayle King, Stedman Graham, Samuel L. Jackson, and A.J Calloway, just to name a few. In March 2015, Kenny opened Gilbert's Underground Kitchen with his wife Anna. Gilbert's Underground Kitchen serves seasonal deep southern cuisine and is located in Fernandina Beach, Florida.
211–215

TOM GRAY
MOXIE KITCHEN + COCKTAILS

Born in Virginia and raised in Orange Park, Florida, Chef Tom Gray graduated from the Culinary Institute of America in Hyde Park, New York and honed his craft in notable kitchens in New York City, Los Angeles, and the Napa Valley before returning to Jacksonville to establish his professional roots. In 2013 he opened Moxie Kitchen + Cocktails, serving his signature take on contemporary regional American cuisine, influenced from his southern upbringing and passion for sustainable sourcing. Among many accolades, Gray has received two James Beard: Best Chef South nominations and was featured in the 2015 James Beard-nominated Tastemade video series, The Grill Iron.
152–157

LIZ GRENAMYER
CATERING BY LIZ GRENAMYER

Liz Grenamyer set out in the culinary world 30 years ago, when she opened her first restaurant. Catering by Liz Grenamyer was established in 1993 as a way for Liz to share her attention to detail and innovative menus in a personal, one-on-one relationship with each client. Catering by Liz is dedicated to offering a team of talented professionals experienced in delivering fine cuisine, extravagant décor, and extraordinary service for every occasion, from small corporate banquets to large weddings. A guiding philosophy of honesty and integrity lies at the heart of Catering by Liz Grenamyer, and above all, passion sets her company apart from the competition. Liz considers each successful party her greatest professional success—at least until the next successful party draws to a close.
57–60

DANIEL GROSHELL
OCEAN 60

Chef Daniel Groshell is Owner & Executive Chef of Ocean 60 Restaurant in Atlantic Beach, Florida. He was born and raised in Jacksonville. Chef Daniel graduated from the Culinary Institute of America in Hyde Park, New York, and opened Ocean 60 in 2001. One of his main culinary influences was his mother, who was a master entertainer, artist, and founder of the local chapter of the Children's International Summer Villages Organization. Chef Daniel had the opportunity to travel with his family to various parts of Europe and Central/South America, where he was exposed to different cultures and cuisines from a very young age. With diverse cooking opportunities and positions from Hawaii to New York, he has been involved in cooking and culinary arts mostly all of his life. In his household, it was a way of life. He incorporates global flavors into each dish he creates and

specifically embraces coastal cuisine using fresh flavors and his foundational French classical techniques.
110–114

RICHARD HAUGK
SUPER FOOD AND BREW

Chef/Partner Richard Haugk is a long-time Jacksonville resident and a graduate of the Culinary Institute of the South. He's worked in some of the finest restaurants in Jacksonville, but truly honed his skills during his eight years as sous chef at Marker 32, a warm, high-end eatery on the Intracoastal Waterway that specializes in locally-sourced seafood. An avid and competitive surfer, Richard knows that healthy, fresh food does not have to be simple. His mother is a world-class Italian cook and his father is an eclectic adventurer in the kitchen: both have helped shape Richard's passion and purpose as a chef.
118–121

JOSEPH HEGLAND
JJ'S BISTRO

I started cooking in high school, mostly desserts as a way to get attention from girls. After studying a number of subjects in college, it became clear that cooking was my passion. I consider my style that of a mad scientist: combining flavors from one dish with techniques from another, and constantly trying new ways to make the staple dishes. For the last nine years, I have been a chef with JJ's Bistro. I enjoy the challenges it presents as well as the freedom to make my own dishes. Our wine dinners are easily my favorite part because of the level of control I have over the entire meal. If I had any advice for someone following my path it would be to learn guitar; cooking is completely useless while dating.
158–162

CHRIS IRVIN
THE CHEF'S GARDEN CATERING & EVENTS and CUMMER CAFÉ

Chris started washing dishes at an Italian restaurant at 15 to save some money to buy a car. Little did he know, he would discover his passion for food and hospitality working these jobs. After college, he decided to make a career out of food and enrolled in culinary school. He is now the Executive Catering Chef at The Chef's Garden and is a creative collaborator for the company. His food philosophy has always been about simple foods with big flavors, and he has an innate ability to take sophisticated flavors and make them approachable. While his career has afforded him the opportunity to cook for United States Presidents, international dignitaries, and numerous celebrities, his passion lies in delivering extraordinary food to everyday people. He loves food, gardening, travel, and spending time with his wife Tiffany, their 2 pups, and 4 cats.
147–151

HOWARD KIRK
13 GYPSIES

Howard Kirk is Chef/Proprietor of 13 Gypsies Peasant Kitchen in the Riverside area of Jacksonville, Florida. He was raised in the kitchen of Chef Antonio Gomez in Andalucia, Spain. Although he is a self-taught chef, his mother gave him a foundation in cooking. His childhood gave him a love for developing flavors and a healthy respect for tradition. He says, "Without tradition you do not know where you come from and you will not understand where you are going. Tradition lets you make the choice of wanting to innovate or preserve. It's a very powerful thing." Chef Howard still works the line every night of service and heads up the extensive charcuterie program at 13 Gypsies.
268–271

RICK LAUGHLIN
SALT RESTAURANT

Chef de Cuisine Rick Laughlin was born and raised in Cleveland, Ohio. His love for food led him to culinary school at The Le Cordon Bleu, Scottsdale, Arizona. After graduation, he joined the Hyatt Regency Scottsdale followed by the Hyatt Regency Grand Cayman. In 2002, Rick joined The Ritz-Carlton, Amelia Island where he held various positions in the hotel. In 2006, he joined the opening team for The AAA Five Diamond Salt Restaurant located in the hotel. In 2010, Rick took over as Chef de Cuisine and continues to strive for perfection. Rick is redefining contemporary American cuisine with his philosophy of keeping flavors familiar and most importantly, keeping the integrity of the ingredients. Chef Rick's innovative ideas, contemporary techniques, and integration of salts from around the world have taken Salt Restaurant to new heights.
172–176

MICHAEL LUGO
MICHAEL'S TASTING ROOM

Michael is the Executive Chef and Owner of Michael's Tasting Room. MTR opened in 2006, and has been one of the leaders of the culinary scene in St. Augustine. The restaurant focuses on innovative cuisine with a Spanish flair. The restaurant changes its menu seasonally to allow for the use of the freshest ingredients Florida has to offer. Michael got his inspiration from his grandmother in Puerto Rico, but began his culinary dreams in Dallas, Texas. There he worked with many chefs who helped develop his vision. He moved to St. Augustine to pursue a slower pace of life, and to make his dream of opening his own restaurant a reality.
246–249

IAN LYNCH
BISTRO AIX and OVINTE

Ian fell in love with cooking at the age of 10 while helping his mother and grandfather prepare holiday meals. He received a degree in Hotel and Restaurant Management from Northern Arizona State University and a degree in the culinary arts from Johnson & Wales University in Denver. Ian landed an internship at Bistro AIX in Jacksonville working under award-winning chef Tom Gray and worked his way up to Executive Sous Chef. From there he spent time as a consultant, but returned to the kitchen as Executive Chef at The Chef's Garden catering company. Ian is currently the Executive Chef of both Ovinte and Bistro AIX, and brings his worldly knowledge and trained expertise to both kitchens, using fresh, seasonal, (and whenever possible) organic ingredients to create unique and tempting plates. He enjoys surfing and spending time with his family. Ian and his wife Ashley have three children: Liam, Sawyer, and Roan.
65–69, 70–74

GENIE McNALLY
THE FLORIDIAN

Genie McNally is a native Floridian whose family's agricultural roots go back seven generations. She draws much of her culinary inspiration from local food sources and traditions, and reinterprets these into dishes that bring indigenous foods new relevance while still respecting their origins. She is the chef and co-owner (along with her husband, Jeff) of The Floridian restaurant in St. Augustine, which has been the recipient of accolades from many national media sources - notably Southern Living (which made her mama especially proud), Emeril's Florida, Travel & Leisure, NBC News, and USA Today. They are members of Slow Food First Coast and participants in their annual events.
222–226

DAVID MEDURE
RESTAURANT MEDURE

David Medure is co-owner of M Hospitality, a trio of award-winning restaurants and a catering operation: Matthew's, M Shack, and Restaurant Medure. David is a self-taught chef favoring classical French techniques. His fascination with food began in the family's Pennsylvania catering business. As a waiter at The Ritz-Carlton, Amelia Island, he paid his dues and honed his craft on his days off by working in the restaurant's kitchen under the tutelage of his brother, Matthew, the executive chef. His talents got him a job, and the brothers' restaurant empire commenced. They launched Matthew's San Marco with David as chef de cuisine then opened Restaurant Medure, his signature restaurant. David has been featured on Great Chefs of the South, the Golf Channel, and at numerous food festivals and is listed in Best Chefs America.
101–104

MATTHEW MEDURE
MATTHEW'S

Chef Matthew Medure is co-owner of M Hospitality, a trio of award-winning restaurants and a catering company: Matthew's, M Shack, and Restaurant Medure. Matthew's culinary calling was fueled by growing up in the family's catering business in Pennsylvania. After graduating from the Pennsylvania Institute for the Culinary Arts, his meteoric rise began in the kitchen at The Ritz-Carlton, Buckhead. His talent catapulted him to Chef of The Grill at The Ritz-Carlton, Amelia Island where he steered the team to win Florida Trend's Golden Spoon and AAA Five Diamond Awards. Accolades include a stage at Hotel de Paris, Monte Carlo, twice nominated for James Beard Rising Star Chef of the Year, numerous television appearances, as well as being listed in Best Chefs America.

He and his brother, David, are a culinary force in Jacksonville.
230–235

SHELDON MILLETT
SALT RESTAURANT

Born in Niagara-On-The-Lake Ontario, Canada, Sheldon Millett spent his childhood years assisting his mother in the kitchen. Chef Sheldon started his young career at The Pillar & Post as a dishwasher and slowly moved his way up to an overnight baker. From there he moved to Toronto and started his tour around the world to expand his expertise through culinary cultural immersion, spending seven years with The Four Seasons. As Executive Pastry Chef at The Ritz-Carlton, Amelia Island since 2002, Sheldon leads the development and execution of all pastry offerings for all food and beverage outlets and an active banquet kitchen. Sheldon has won numerous culinary awards and was selected to develop three recipes for *Classic Desserts Redefined at The Ritz-Carlton*. In his personal time, Sheldon enjoys spending time with his wife, Stacy, and two children, Mackenzie and Nicholas. His hobbies include running, yoga, and just enjoying island life on Amelia Island.
35–39

CELESTIA MOBLEY
POTTER'S HOUSE SOUL FOOD BISTRO

As general manager of The Potter's House Soul Food Bistro, Executive Chef Celestia Mobley has turned what began as the church's food services ministry into the most successful soul food restaurant in Jacksonville. Celeste (as she is affectionately known) began cooking at the tender age of eight, learning from her maternal grandmother, who she watched prepare family dinners with love. In 1998, upon leaving a 10-year career in banking, Celeste opened Lojope's Seafood Restaurant, specializing in the Southern favorite garlic

crabs and shrimp. In 1999, Celeste sold the seafood restaurant and became head cook at the Potter's House Café. Upon her graduation from FCCJ's Culinary School with a degree in Culinary Management in 2002, Celeste left the café for a brief stint to complete an internship at The River Club. She later returned to the café as restaurant manager, and the café expanded to The Soul Food Bistro in 2007. Celeste serves on the board of The American Culinary Federation and participates in the Chef and Child Program. In 2009, Celeste earned the classification of Certified Executive Chef through ACF. Celeste resides in Bryceville, Florida with her husband, Varon and their daughter, Jasmine.
20-25

BRIAN MOORE
13 GYPSIES

Brian Moore is Sous Chef/Proprietor of 13 Gypsies Peasant Kitchen. Brian began at a young age as a dishwasher and eventually made the transition to the front of the house as a server. For some insane reason he made the choice to cook. He wanted to join the legion of cooks who came before him and the tradition of long hours, little pay, burns, cuts, and back pain. His hard work and high standards have given Chef Howard the freedom to oversee the future and direction of the small bistro. Brian is the heart and soul of the pasta program at 13 Gypsies, and without his stubborn pursuit of great pasta, the recipe in this book would not be as good as it is.
268-271

DEBBIE AND DON NICOL
TACOLU

Debbie and Don Nicol came into the restaurant business later than most. They opened the first Sticky Fingers in Florida after years of working in the retail industry. Debbie has always been in the "Art World"—starting with a degree from the Art Institute in Ft. Lauderdale, then in the framing and art supply business in Chattanooga, Tennessee and then Charleston, South Carolina. Don never had a restaurant job until after he graduated from Jacksonville University, when, much to the chagrin of his father, he moved to Nashville to be in a rock band, while tending to the salad bar at Ruby Tuesday during the daytime! From there it was retail furniture in Charleston until his friends from Chattanooga, the Sticky Fingers boys, came calling in 1998! The rest is, as they say, kinda boring...
93-96

KATIE RIEHM
SWEET THEORY BAKING CO.

Katie Riehm is the owner of Sweet Theory Baking Co., a bakery specializing in all-natural and organic allergen-friendly treats. A Jacksonville native, Katie began her education at UNF. When it became apparent she would have to complete the math courses she had spent years avoiding, she took it as a sign. She left to pursue her passion for natural foods and the culinary arts at The Natural Gourmet Institute in New York City. She graduated in 2010 and returned to Jacksonville with the vision to start an alternative bakery, opening Sweet Theory in 2012.
88-92

WAYLON RIVERS
BLACK SHEEP RESTAURANT

Waylon Rivers is the Executive Chef of Black Sheep Restaurant, a modern American restaurant that has earned numerous accolades from local and regional publications since opening in 2012. Rivers is a graduate of Florida State College at Jacksonville's Culinary Institute of the South, where he studied Culinary Management. Prior to his arrival at Black Sheep, Rivers was the Sous Chef of Georges Brasserie in Charlotte, North Carolina. His background also includes time spent in the kitchens of Restaurant Orsay and The Capital Grille in Jacksonville.
132-136

KEVIN SBRAGA
SBRAGA & COMPANY

Chef Kevin Sbraga is the chef-owner of Sbraga Dining and winner of Bravo's "Top Chef: Season 7." In 2008, Sbraga worked with Jose Garces to recipe test for Garces' *Latin Evolution* cookbook, ultimately becoming Culinary Director of Garces Group. Sbraga went on to win Best Meat Presentation in the Bocuse d'Or USA culinary competition in 2008, before working as Executive Chef for Stephen Starr at Rat's Restaurant at the Grounds for Sculpture. In 2010, Sbraga joined the cast of "Top Chef." Soon after taking home the title of Top Chef, Sbraga launched his modern American restaurant, Sbraga, in 2011, named one of Esquire's "Best New Restaurant" in 2012. His second venture, The Fat Ham, opened in 2013, serving small plates of Southern comfort food. His newest concept, Sbraga & Company, a contemporary approach to the cultural influences of Northeast Florida, opened its doors in 2015.
259-262

SCOTT SCHWARTZ
29 SOUTH

Scott Schwartz is Executive Chef and Owner of 29 South. Chef Schwartz's accomplishments include serving as Executive Chef at some of Atlanta's best restaurants, as food stylist for National Pork Producers Council during the 1995 World Expo, and as a featured chef during the 1996 Olympic Games festivities. In 1998, he was ranked by Gourmet magazine as one of the top 25 chefs in Atlanta. In 2004, Chef Schwartz cooked for the James Beard House and Foundation. Throughout his career, Schwartz has earned several culinary awards

and is a member of the prestigious Les Toques Blanches. He was awarded Folio Magazine Best Chef Jacksonville in 2007 and 2008. Considered one of Jacksonville's pioneers in the region's farm-to-fork movement, in 2009, 29 South was awarded the Spirit of Slow Food Award and a Snail of Approval. From 2010-2013, Florida Trend Magazine awarded 29 South the coveted Golden Spoon. In 2011, his Coffee and Doughnuts dessert was given the title of one of the "South's 50 Best Dishes" in Garden and Gun magazine, and 29 South was featured in the book *A Southern Foodies Guide: 100 Places You Should Eat before You Die*. Currently, Chef Schwartz serves on the International Advisory Board for the Florida WineFest as Culinary Chairman. He is also a co-founder of The Legend Series.
236–240

CHASON SPENCER
HOPTINGER

My background as a cook started when I was a young boy. I learned to love food and cooking with my father and grandmother and all of the non-written recipes they taught me. I went to culinary school right out of high school and graduated two weeks after turning 21. I learned a lot of French technique and plating from Restaurant Orsay, where perfection is an every-day occurrence. Now at Hoptinger, I work with a lot of beers and sausage but we use high quality products and make almost everything from scratch or source here locally in Jacksonville. Pairing beers with food is an up-and-coming niche, and I am glad I get to be a part of it.
207–210

JEFFREY STANFORD
THE BLIND RABBIT, A BURGER AND WHISKEY BAR

Chef Jeffrey Stanford places a strong emphasis on Southern cooking influenced by a Southern Creole heritage. His passion for Southern cuisine, creole flavors, and farm-to-table food along with the use of fresh, local ingredients characterize his dishes. His travels across the South led to the embracing of different cultures and cuisines of these Southern coastal areas.
163–166

TOBEN STUBEE
5LOAVES 2FISH MOBILE KITCHEN FOOD TRUCK

After growing up in Miami and being exposed to Latin and Caribbean cuisines, I became interested in pursuing a career in the restaurant industry. Fast forward 25 years and my experiences range from fast food, corporate, fine dining, and private residence chef. I have a bachelor's degree from The Culinary Institute of America in Restaurant Operations and was the valedictorian for both the culinary program and business management program. I have worked in restaurants in Miami, New York, Orlando, Jacksonville, and St. Augustine. Locally, I was the chef at Opus 39, Matthew's, and Eleven South, which I opened and which received "Best New Restaurant" within 6 months. For the past six years I have been a private chef for a husband/wife who own a national clothing store. Opening the 5Loaves 2Fish Mobile Kitchen food truck is an exciting opportunity to cook fresh, creative, and inspired foods and be able to interact with customers on a face-to-face basis.
97–100

DAVEN WARDYNSKI
OMNI AMELIA ISLAND PLANTATION

Executive Chef Daven Wardynski has led the culinary team at Omni Amelia Island Plantation since October 2012, overseeing nine restaurants as well as conference food operations. With more than 23 years of experience in the culinary world, Wardynski began his career at the legendary TRU in Chicago, serving as Sous Chef under celebrity chef Rick Tramonto and also spent time with the infamous Charlie Trotters restaurant, where he learned the importance of quality and refinement. Prior to accepting his current position at Omni Amelia Island Plantation, he was the executive chef at Omni Chicago Hotel and Jean Georges' Pump Room. Due to his Midwest farm boy roots, his emphasis on supporting the local economy focuses on an unmatched passion for fresh, quality ingredients. This has led to Chef Wardynski being recognized by Food & Wine, Travel + Leisure, Star Chefs, USA Today, and Oprah for redefining the artisan tastes of his locale.
189–193

CALLI WEBB
BREW FIVE POINTS

With a passion for making people happy with the sweeter things in life, Calli Webb has made serious waves in the Jacksonville food scene during her five short years as a professional baker. A recent graduate in Culinary Business Management from the Arts Institute of Jacksonville, she currently manages the food program for BREW Five Points, where she develops delicious weekly specials to complement specialty coffee and craft beer.
250–253

MARLON HALL
CANDY APPLE CAFÉ

A Circle in the Square Theater School graduate, former actor, and self-described bourbon lover, Marlon Hall became accidentally enamored with bartending when he jumped in to cover someone's shift. He only planned to bartend to fill time between gigs, but he got hooked once he understood the relationship between food and booze. He's a fan of balanced flavors and likes to use a lot of bitters, bold whiskeys, and cool, savory ingredients. He is revolutionizing the cocktail scene in our city and is proud to be one of the initial members of the Jacksonville chapter of the United States Bartenders' Guild. Marlon is known equally for his dapper dressing as for his skills behind the bar. When he's not crafting cocktails, you can find him sharing sartorial insight with local food and entertainment blogs.

44–47, 48

ZACH LYNCH
THE ICE PLANT

After bartending in Orlando for a little over 10 years in different formats from fine dining to microbrews and craft cocktails, I helped found the Central Florida Chapter of the United States Bartenders Guild. While working an event in Miami, I met the owners of The Ice Plant and St. Augustine Distillery and decided to relinquish my position as the President of the USBG and bar manager position at Prato in Winter Park. I took on the beverage program at The Ice Plant and later became Brand Ambassador for the St. Augustine Distillery, where I helped head of production Brendan Wheatley, develop the gold-medal-winning New World Gin.

44–47, 49

BLAIR REDINGTON
THE PARLOUR AT GRAPE AND GRAIN EXCHANGE

I was born and raised in the San Marco area and graduated from Bishop Kenny. I worked at Bistro Aix from 2002 to 2012 before my passion for craft spirits and cocktails led me down San Marco Boulevard to Grape and Grain Exchange in 2013. I love being able to use fresh ingredients and source things locally when allowed.

44–47, 49

KURT ROGERS
SIDECAR

Kurt W. Rogers II was born in Portsmouth, Virginia. He has been in the bartending business for more than 20 years and currently works at Sidecar and Flask & Cannon. Kurt has also held positions at Orsay, Black Sheep, and Fly's Tie. His favorite quote is: "Share your knowledge. It is a way to achieve mortality." - Dalai Lama

44–47, 50

CASEY SHELTON
DOS GATOS

When it comes to cocktails, Jacksonville Magazine and Folio Weekly's 2014 Best Bartender Casey Shelton is recognized widely as one of the top in his craft. His strong culinary background shows in his drink making, but beyond that it is about having fun. Never one to take himself too seriously (he has been known to work the odd shift dressed fully like Beetlejuice or Hell Boy), at the end of the day, making cocktails that are approachable and crowd pleasing is where he is in the zone. As Bar Manager of Dos Gatos Downtown and EverBank, he has been bringing killer cocktails to the masses for almost five years while never losing focus on quality, attention to detail, and the overall guest experience. Whether you are looking for a properly-made vintage cocktail, something new and exciting, or simply a bomb shot and bad decisions, you have found your man.

44–47, 48

AARDWOLF

Aardwolf is a production brewery and tap room located in a historic ice house nestled in the heart of San Marco. We brew beers ranging from traditional German and Belgian styles to heavily hoppy American-style beers as well as barrel-aged stouts and sours. Our guiding principle is to make beer we would want to drink and to spare no effort or expense to make the best beer possible.

81–83, 84

BOLD CITY BREWERY

Locally owned and operated, Bold City Brewery was created by the mother/son team of Susan and Brian Miller. They both became dissatisfied with the corporate world and decided to join the beer biz in 2008. Brian began home brewing in 2002 and crafted what would become Bold City's signature brands. Susan uses her corporate knowledge and runs the business side of the brewery while Brian heads the brewery operations. The rest of the Miller family, with the help from friends and relatives, all have a hand in the day-to-day operations. Bold City Brewery is truly a family-owned and -operated brewery.

81–83, 84

ENGINE 15 BREWING CO.

Engine 15 Brewing Co. is one of Jacksonville's first craft breweries. Born of two beer lovers with a passion for brewing and sharing great beers, Engine 15 enjoys a loyal following at both the original Jacksonville Beach location and the new production facility in downtown Jacksonville, where the current offering of year-round beers are brewed for both in-house sale as well as distribution.

81–83, 85

GREEN ROOM BREWING

Green Room Brewing gives you a reason to ditch the surfboard and pull up a stool at Jacksonville Beach's first craft brewery! Their goal is to bring great, locally made beer to the Beaches and beyond. At Green Room, they brew beers that interest the casual drinker and the beer aficionado.

81–83, 85

INTUITION ALE WORKS

Intuition Ale Works is a Jacksonville, Florida-based craft brewery established in 2010. They specialize in small-batch handcrafted ales with a mission to create quality, flavorful, and creative beers in a wide range of styles. In 2012, Intuition became the first craft brewery in the state of Florida to can their beers, and the brewery is currently canning four brands: the flagship People's Pale Ale, Jon Boat Coastal Ale, I-10 IPA, and King Street Stout. They also brew a host of draught-only small batch specialties that can be found in their tap room and at better beer bars in Florida.

81–83, 86

PINGLEHEAD BREWING COMPANY

Pinglehead Brewing Company craftsmen make BIG BEER, full of flavor with the best ingredients money can buy. They call it "Beer with Attitude!" and are committed to creating beer that will always be made with quality ingredients and our strong commitment to the craft! It will never be rushed.

81–83, 86

VETERANS UNITED CRAFT BREWERY

Veterans United Craft Brewery is owned by military veterans who share an enthusiastic desire for producing and enjoying quality craft beer. They offer a variety of delicious ales, which are available on tap by the pint and in take-home growlers and kegs from their taproom located in the heart of Baymeadows/Southside at the end of Western Way. The brewery's founder, Ron Gamble, is a former Naval Flight Officer, and has been a brewer in the craft brewing industry since 2007 and a passionate homebrewer since 1999. Ron's vision is to take the same spirit, pride, and dedication of his military service and infuse this energy into a company that creates great-tasting and innovative craft beers.

81–83, 87

ZETA BREWING COMPANY

Located in the heart of Jacksonville Beach, Zeta Brewing creates traditional American ales and lagers just steps away from the sand. Signature beers include the American Garage IPA, Private Rye, Power to the Porter, Ruby Beach Wheat, and Twin Finn Lager. The brewery also creates original seasonals that are rotated throughout the year. On top of a great brewery and patio, Zeta Brewing also holds a full liquor bar and kitchen. With local craft beer, brunch, dinner specials, and live music on weekends, Zeta Brewing has something for everyone.

81–83, 87

Quotations originally appeared in the following: [1] From an unpublished email in the Cummer Museum Archives, April 4, 2014. [2] Stuart Jeffries, "The Saturday interview: Howard Hodgkin at 80," *Guardian*, July 27, 2012. [3] Quoted in a letter dated February 17, 1885 from Eugène Charvot to his niece from the Cummer Museum Archives. [4] Quoted in Timothy Kennedy, *Richard Protovin: Landscapes of the Mind*, 531 Central Fine Arts, St. Petersburg, Florida.

Emily Moody
Project Manager

After stints in Dallas, Los Angeles, and Atlanta, Emily Moody was passionate about moving back to Jacksonville to help create a vibrant arts and culture scene in her hometown. Emily's knack for innovative business concepts is apparent through her founding of the award-winning live music venue, Underbelly. There, she brought hundreds of national and international acts to the stage in Jacksonville. Currently, she continues to nurture Jacksonville's cultural scene in her position as Public Program Manager at the Cummer Museum of Art & Gardens, where she creates innovative Museum events and programs that attract a wide range of demographics.

Holly Keris
Art Copywriter

Holly Keris is the Chief Curator at the Cummer Museum of Art & Gardens. She received undergraduate degrees in History and Humanities from Stetson University in DeLand, Florida, and a graduate degree in the History of Art from the University of Virginia. Holly has been with the Cummer Museum since 2003, where she strives to bring the Museum's Permanent Collection, exhibitions, and historic gardens to life for the broader community.

Varick Rosete
Designer

Varick Rosete is an award-winning designer and illustrator, creating great experiences for local heroes and worldwide clients, with his expertise expanding from advertising to web/app developement to video production and animation. Varick is an avid supporter for the designer and design thinking, and is a proud member of AIGA, the professional association for design, serving as President for the Jacksonville Chapter from 2009 through 2011. Additionally, Varick's entrepreneurial spirit has been integral in the development of several companies including fashion startup Wolf & Cub, Filipino-based clothing line Tsinilas Clothing Company, interactive agency nGen Works, collaborative community hotspot CoWork Jax, and co-founding the World's Crowdfunding Festival One Spark. Driven to create something new and fresh, Varick is always learning, especially when it involves ideation and visualization.

Cari Sánchez-Potter
Project Manager

Cari Sánchez-Potter is a culinary entrepreneur based in Jacksonville, Florida. She is the owner of a food-focused event production and consulting company, trained gastronomist, award-winning cookbook author, and food writer.

Cari was awarded the Arts Innovator honor by the Cultural Council of Greater Jacksonville for breaking new ground and elevating Jacksonville's culinary culture through her business The Legend Series. Her first cookbook, Cooking with Intuition, features recipes using beer from craft brewery Intuition Ale Works and won multiple national independent publishing and design awards. She has contributed food articles to many publications.

Cari holds a Bachelor of Science in Marketing from Boston College and a Master of Arts in Gastronomy from The University of Adelaide / Le Cordon Bleu in South Australia. Her experience living on five different continents has informed her approach to the local cultural initiatives she spearheads.

Agnes Lopez
Photographer

Agnes Lopez is an editorial and food photographer with a home base in Jacksonville, Florida's historic Riverside-Avondale neighborhood. Agnes traverses the Southeastern US and beyond with her camera in search of inspiration in the form of exceptional meals, her subjects ranging from the fine cuisine of award-winning restaurants to food trucks and their street fare. Her work appears regularly in the pages of food and lifestyle publications across the US.

The Cummer Museum of Art & Gardens holds one of the finest art collections in the Southeast, with nearly 5,000 objects in its Permanent Collection. The Museum offers world-class art spanning from 2100 B.C. through the 21st century, features diverse special exhibits, and is home to the Wark Collection of Early Meissen Porcelain.

The Museum's 2.5 acres of historic gardens are unique examples of early 20th century garden design, featuring reflecting pools, fountains, arbors, antique ornaments, and sculptures. The majestic Cummer Oak has a canopy of more than 150 feet and is one of the oldest trees in Jacksonville.

Art Connections, the Museum's nationally recognized interactive education center, enhances the cultural learning of visitors of all ages by offering educational programs and interactive opportunities, both in and out of the Museum, allowing visitors to gain a better understanding of works in the Collection.